S0-ADZ-398

Training the Boy's Changing Voice

84,96
119 7
MT
915
M2

Training the Boy's Changing Voice

8549

DUNCAN McKENZIE, M.A., *Edinburgh*

RUTGERS UNIVERSITY PRESS
New Brunswick, New Jersey · · **1956**

Copyright © 1956

By the Trustees of Rutgers College in New Jersey

Library of Congress Catalogue Card Number: 56-7611

Manufactured in the United States of America

by Quinn & Boden Company, Inc., Rahway, New Jersey

To

RIGHT REVEREND MONSIGNOR LAWRENCE H. BRACKEN,
Founder and Conductor of the Catholic Diocesan Choir, Brooklyn,
New York, and the boys of his choir

Preface

The problem of the adolescent boy's voice has received a great deal of attention in America because of the music program that has been evolved in the junior high school. The problem has been discussed at many music educators conferences; many articles have been written about it; and books on music in the junior high school always take note of it in a general way. Compilers and editors of music texts designed to meet the conditions of boys' changing voices usually review the topic in their prefatory remarks on the types of arrangements they consider possible for voices in the junior high school. Even so, there are very few books which deal specifically with the modern theory concerning the boy voice. This is the more surprising since the boy's changing voice is equally a problem for the choirmaster, who, because he must think in terms of replacements to fill vacancies in the men's sections of his choir, wants to keep the boy who has been in the junior choir interested in singing during the adolescent period.

To a great extent, the editorials from American and English music journals quoted in the first chapter suggested the idea of the book and what its scope should be. At the outset, the traditional theory about the boy voice—the English viewpoint—is compared with the modern theory—the American viewpoint. The latter has resulted in the evolution of the alto-tenor plan of dealing with the boy's voice during the mutation stage, a plan that is peculiar to America and a product of its junior high school music program. Although mention will be made of other plans, the theme of the book throughout is the alto-tenor plan. This is described in an exhaustive way.

The discussion of training the boy's changing voice by the alto-tenor plan under classroom conditions is the result of many years of experience in teaching school music in Scotland and Canada, and of observation and consultation with teachers in different parts of America. Since the most satisfactory way of studying the development of the boy's changing voice during the adolescent period is to keep individual voice histories, one chapter is devoted to a selection of typical voice histories. Because of the scarcity of tenors in the high school and the adult choir, special attention is given to methods of preserving the pre-tenor voice.

Part Two describes other plans in current use, both here and abroad, that follow the modern theory about the boy voice. Plans which have been worked out for school purposes include the "non-choir" plan of a famous English public school and a six-part classification for the mixed chorus of a New Zealand high school. Also described are the counter-tenor, the baritone, and the multiple choir plans developed by church musicians who believe in the modern theory; the last plan has been gaining favor in the music programs of many American churches.

Duncan McKenzie

Mattapoisett, Massachusetts
April 1955

Acknowledgments

I wish to acknowledge my indebtedness to the following choirmasters whose cooperation made it possible to describe their methods of dealing with adolescent boys' voices according to the modern theory: Monsignor Lawrence H. Bracken, founder of the Cathedral Diocesan Choir of Brooklyn, who permitted me to attend his choir rehearsals and test the boys' voices over a period of three years in order to observe the working of the baritone plan; William Ripley Dorr, St. Luke's Church, Long Branch, California, who enabled me, through correspondence, to present a description of his way of using the counter-tenor plan; Donald C. Gilley, formerly Minister of Music, Wesley Methodist Church, Worcester, Massachusetts, who gave permission to make use of a paper read at a convention of the American Guild of Organists; H. William Hawke, formerly organist and choirmaster, St. Mark's Church, Philadelphia, who, after allowing me to observe his work with his choirboys, wrote to me at length about the procedure followed in his Junior Choirmen's Class; Arthur Leslie Jacobs, formerly Minister of Music, First Congregational Church of Los Angeles, who wrote to me at length about his philosophy concerning the Young Men's Ensemble in his multiple choir plan; Federal Whittlesey, Minister of Music, Highland Park Methodist Church, Dallas, Texas, who granted permission to use quotations from an article describing his Young People's Choir, a unit of the multiple choir plan.

To the many music educators and officials with whom I exchanged views while preparing this book I express my deep appreciation:

On the origin of the term "alto-tenor," and the first use of the alto-tenor plan in the early days of school music in America, invaluable information was supplied me by the late Ralph Baldwin, Director of Music, Hartford, Connecticut, schools, the late Eldridge Newton, music editor for Ginn and Company, and the late Leo R. Lewis, of Tufts College.

I wish to thank Will Earhart, formerly Director of Music, Pittsburgh schools, and Jacob Evanston, Supervisor of Choral Music, Pittsburgh, for their comments on a comparison of the music arrangements for adolescent voices used in American and English schools. Quotations from an article by the late Mr. G. Kirkham Jones, headmaster of a London County Council School, relating his experiences with children evacuated from London during World War II, are given here by permission of Mrs. Jones. Thanks are due also to Mary H. Kiess, Haven School, Evanston, Illinois, for her comments on the first basses of her boys' glee club; and to Gertrude M. Scott, Head of the Music Department, Harding Junior High School, Lakewood, Ohio, for keeping voice histories and observing the changing voices of boys in her glee club.

For a description of the six-part voice classification evolved in a New Zealand high school, Vernon Griffiths, Professor of Music, Canterbury University College, Christchurch, New Zealand, kindly allowed me to make use of materials in his book, *An Experiment in School Music-Making*. The chapter on Oundle School, England, is based on two articles by the late Clement M. Spurling, Director of Music at Oundle. Mr. Spurling discussed with me the various points in his plan, and read and approved the chapter on the choral program at Oundle. R. Vaughan Williams gave kind permission to quote from a letter describing the singing of the massed chorus at Oundle.

For statements of current British and Canadian attitudes on the boy voice question, I am indebted to G. Roy Fenwick, Director of Music, Ontario Department of Education, Toronto; Cyril Winn, formerly H.M. Staff Inspector of Music in Schools, Ministry of Education, London; and Herbert Wiseman, formerly Director of Music, Public Schools, Edinburgh.

D. M. K.

Contents

Part One

Part Two

Part One

· 1 ·

The Boy Voice Question: Traditional versus Modern Theory

How to deal with the adolescent boy's singing voice has long been a subject for controversy and practical concern in church and public school music circles. In England, the traditional, or "break," theory handed down by centuries of cathedral choirmasters holds that the boy's voice breaks during adolescence and that once this occurs the boy should refrain from singing until such time as his voice has developed into tenor or bass. For most boys, this period is, roughly, from two to three years, or, in other words, the period covered by the seventh to the ninth years of school. This is the theory generally adopted by church musicians and school music educators in England and by church musicians in America. Teachers of public school music in America, however, have never accepted the traditional theory, and in recent years its fallibility has been questioned in England.

Even as early as 1885, Emil Behnke and Lennox Browne, the first published spokesmen on the boy voice question in England, recognized two opposing theories. After questioning over two hundred choirmasters and singing teachers and recording the experiences of nearly three hundred students in teacher training colleges, they concluded that "the bulk of the evidence most strikingly proves the injurious and even ruinous consequences arising from the exercise of the voice by singing during the period of change." They admitted, however, that the boy's voice may change "gradually and imperceptibly," in which case there is no break, and singing "*may* possibly be continued, under the guidance of a competent teacher, without detriment." [1]

The modern theory of the adolescent boy's voice holds that the voice changes gradually and that the boy may sing throughout the period of change provided that he is taught how to use his voice properly.

[1] *The Child's Voice: Its Treatment with Regards to After-Development* (London, Sampson Low, 1885).

Singing is likely to be beneficial rather than injurious, for the voice is kept in action. With careful voice training, the voice is preserved during the period of puberty and the changed voice emerges under favorable conditions.

The question of which theory is right has by no means been settled, but out of individual initiative or practical necessity have come several successful plans and experiments both in England and America. (Some of these, notably the alto-tenor plan, will be described at length in later chapters.) The controversy continues, nevertheless. G. Edward Stubbs, a well-known New York organist and contributor to musical magazines, wrote in 1930: "The mere fact that the subject will not die out proves rather conclusively that it is not one-sided by any means, and that there is plenty of room for information, especially of a scientific kind. Choirmasters who train boys' voices are naturally interested in retaining the 'treble' as long as possible; yet there are few, we believe, who are willing to risk injury in doing so. As a rule boys who show danger of vocal strain are warned to sing very quietly, and leave top notes alone, allowing the voice to take its natural course towards tenor, baritone, or bass. But in a percentage of cases the treble voice never changes at all, and that this represents something unnatural has never been proved to the satisfaction of choirmasters of experience."[2]

Dr. Stubbs was commenting on a symposium which had been conducted that year by *The Music Teacher* (London) on the topic, "Should breaking voices be rested?"[3] Referring to an opinion expressed by Sir Edward Bairstow, Organist of York Minster, that "although boys vary greatly, nevertheless the chorister who uses his voice naturally and without forcing it, never goes through a period when he cannot sing at all," Dr. Stubbs concluded by saying: "As more is known in England about the boy treble than is known in any other country, owing to the practical experience of five centuries with trained voices, the treatment of this subject in the columns of *The Music Teacher* ought to settle the question once for all. The writer believes it is largely a matter of care and expert training on the part of the choirmaster. The average boy voice, if properly handled, will gradually lower without any break whatever. The exceptions to the rule are too few to be taken into account. . . . There is nothing new in the no-break theory; it is as old as the hills. What is needed is more scientific recognition of a fact of importance, and more widespread knowledge concerning it."

[2] *New Music Review* (New York), July 1930. Dr. Stubbs is also the author of *The Adult Male Alto or Counter-Tenor Voice* (New York, H. W. Gray, 1939).

[3] Several eminent British musicians were invited to express their opinions on the question, and the results were published in the April 1930 issue of the magazine.

A British comment on the symposium, which took the form of an editorial in the *Musical Mirror* (London), was quoted as follows by Dr. Stubbs: "In recent years, at odd times, and from varying sources of information, a strong trend has been developing to allow a limited amount of vocal activity during the period of puberty, not only in the case of boys, but also of girls, the argument being that what is so pronounced in the male is identically followed in the female, only in a less strident degree. Naturally there are many differences of opinion on the matter. So far the difficulty has been that musicians, choirmasters, and teachers of singing have mostly favored giving the singing voice a complete rest between the ages of fourteen and seventeen, and this notwithstanding the fact that history, physiology, and the science of phonology—not to speak of practical experience—were all ranged against them. *Grove's Dictionary* teems with the histories of great singers of the past (Santley, Reeves, Lloyd, Patti, Melba), who not only sang throughout the period of adolescence, but who actually owed much of their success to the fact that they never ceased singing from early childhood. . . . One of the most striking peculiarities of the case is, that instead of their voices being damaged, they thrived upon what they were fed; those who had the *nous* to keep on singing did not damage their voices one jot, as is so frequently prognosticated, but on the contrary, built for themselves vocal possibilities that advanced with the flight of ages."

Two years later, a public statement on the side of the traditional theory by Dr. C. H. Moody,[4] Organist of Ripon Cathedral, elicited an editorial by Dr. Harvey Grace in the *Musical Times* (London and New York) for July 1932: "Dr. Moody's pronouncement against the singing of boys for three years after the breaking stage will, I hope, lead to something like a practical finding on the subject. We have to face the fact that every year many hundreds of enthusiastic choirboys end their singing careers forever. It will, I think, be agreed that the majority of these boys stop singing with regret; but during the blank period that follows, they lose their taste for singing and the majority are definitely lost to choral music. If perfect rest could be achieved there might be something to say for Dr. Moody's views, but we know that no power on earth can stop boys from shouting at their games, and from singing raucously at Scouts' camps and other gatherings. It is difficult to see how properly controlled and directed singing during the adolescent period could do a hundredth part of the damage that is done by uncontrolled shouting and yelling. I have heard of choirmasters who have tackled the problem by running a junior choirmen's

[4] Dr. Moody is the author of *The Choir Boy in the Making* (2nd ed., London, Oxford University Press, 1939). He was organist at Ripon Cathedral from 1902 to 1955.

class analogous to that of treble probationers. Perhaps some readers who have had practical experience of this, or any other method of retaining the musical interest of boys during the change-of-voice period, will give other readers the benefit of their experiences. . . . If the present leakage of splendid choral material is unavoidable, there is nothing more to be said; but if the weight of evidence shows that the waste can be stopped, something ought to be done, and done promptly."

Whatever the merits of the opposing theories, there is an obvious conflict between theory and practice insofar as the traditional theory is concerned in choir work, in both England and the United States. The nature of the choirmaster's work and his working conditions are bound to have a great deal to do with his attitude in the matter. He has above all the responsibility of keeping up the standard of work for every Sunday of the year, but his choice of vocal material is limited because the number of boys he can have in the choir is determined by the seating capacity in the chancel of the church. (The average seating is twenty-four.) From the English point of view, the soprano choirboy is a very valuable member of the choir just as he is approaching the adolescent stage. It has taken three or four years to train him, and his voice is now at its best. In choirs of small size, the loss during a year of a few experienced boys who have been the backbone of the soprano section is a serious problem. Since a new boy will not become even an efficient chorister until he has had at least one year's training and experience, the choirmaster must usually try to keep the proportion of older boys and replacements at one to three (or one to two). It is understandable then that he is likely to view signs of adolescence in the boy's physique and speaking voice with alarm. Because his primary concern must be to retain the sopranos of his choir as long as possible, he may see no reason for stopping the boy from singing soprano as long as he is able to sing the part. The choirmaster's problem dwarfs his consideration of what is best for the individual boy at this stage for the sake of his future voice.

But what happens eventually when a boy continues to sing soprano after he has reached the adolescent stage? Sooner or later there comes a time when his voice will break on the highest notes of his range because nature has decreed he should not be singing them. Then the lowest notes become weak, and the longer the boy continues to sing soprano, the weaker the lower notes become. Soon the bottom of the voice "drops out" (in the region of middle C), and he cannot sing the lowest notes of his range. The lower part of the voice has been sacrificed at the expense of the upper. At this stage, the man's voice starts to develop, but until it develops completely, the boy experiences a period when his voice is neither that of a boy nor that of a man, with the break as likely to appear in the upper as in the lower part of the range. With his voice range shortened at both ends, he is no longer of use in the choir as a soprano, and his services must be dispensed with. Because of the way the voice has been used, and because the boy has not yet been trained to find that part of his voice which nature intends him to use at this time—the lower part—this has appeared to be a logical and acceptable sequence of events.

The traditional theory has also been followed until recently in England in the schools; consequently, the boy's voice has never been regarded as a changing one in the sense that the term "changing" is used in school music in America. This is apparent from the fact that the music published for English school use is mainly unison and two-part, as are the test pieces that are selected for competition festivals, although a few of the pieces are three-part. There is evidence that some attention was paid to the adolescent boy bass a half-century ago, for a music book, *Cantemus,* a collection of folk songs arranged for soprano, alto, and bass, was published in London in 1908 (Curwen). It was intended for use in the upper grades of the elementary school where boy basses would be found. For many years this book was the only one of its kind, as far as I have been able to discover. The fact that a second volume was not published until 1929 indicates that there was very little demand for soprano-alto-bass material. In the high schools no choral singing was arranged for boys until their voices had completely changed.

In contrast, the stand that the teacher of school music in America has always taken is that a period of rest is not necessary. If the boy is taught how to use his voice and is properly classified for range he can go on singing throughout the years when his voice is changing. Because of this, the boy is ready to take part in choral work for mixed and male voices at an earlier age than would have been possible if the voice had been rested. It should be remembered, too, that if a boy ceases to sing during adolescence, the chances are great that he may never again take up choral music; he may not be moved to return to it if, during the formative period of voice and character, he is cut off from the physical benefits of singing and the yet unrealized spiritual force of song. Dr. Will Earhart, while he was Director of Music in the schools of Pittsburgh, Pennsylvania, remarked: "Continuation of general musical training and experience plus the habit of singing is what should be emphasized. Discontinuance of vocal practice seems hardly so serious to me as discontinuance of aural and general musical preoccupation. As you know, I have always emphasized in my own thought preoccupying the mind with tonal and musical imagery. I depart further each year from the conception of music as something that exists only when the air is vibrating."

Edward Birge in his *History of Public School Music in the United States* (rev. ed., New York, Oliver Ditson, 1937) tells about the early days of music in the high school towards the end of the nineteenth century before the junior high school came into existence. "In 1880 Samuel Cole gave what was probably the first rendition of a complete oratorio with a high school chorus. This was a performance of the *Creation* at Dedham, Massachusetts, with orchestra and eminent soloists. In 1891 this was followed by a performance of the *Messiah.* Two years later, in 1893, at Moline, Illinois, Thaddeus P. Giddings gave the *Creation* with a high school chorus of one hundred fifty voices—the entire membership of the school—the bass and soprano solos being taken by the pupils, and the tenor solos by the director." Birge also mentions two performances of the *Creation* in 1903, one at Somerville, Massachusetts, under S. Henry Hadley, and the other at Northampton, Massachusetts, under Ralph Baldwin. "Early in the century a large number of high schools were preparing and performing such works as Cowen's *Rose Maiden,* Gaul's *Holy City* and *Ruth.* . . . These choral accomplishments were not limited to any one section of the country. They were widely scattered, and in some cases the high school chorus was reinforced by adult voices. The performances were regarded as the crowning fulfilment of the work of the grades."

Only boys with changed voices could have taken part in these performances; the problem of the changing voice did not concern the high school music teacher of that time. However, with the birth of the junior high school at the beginning of the twentieth century, the boy voice question had to be faced, for music was a part of the curriculum. But there was no music available to suit the voice conditions of boys of junior high school age. Two books intended specifically for mixed classes in the junior high school were issued within four years of each other: *The Laurel Music Reader,* edited by W. L. Tomlins, in 1914 (Boston, Birchard), and *Junior Songs,* by Hollis Dann, in 1918 (New York, American Book). Both books came to be widely used.

The preface to *Junior Songs* reveals what the American viewpoint towards the boy voice was. It states that the book was "designed for use in schools where changing voices introduce peculiar problems. To meet this situation a large amount of material has been specially composed or arranged, with optional parts for changed voices. The special treatment thus demanded, has resulted in the division of the book into five parts, each of which with the exception of Part Five contributes to the solution of the problem of voice distribution." An examination of the contents shows the five parts to be as follows:

Part I: Material for unchanged voices in unison, two, and three parts, some with and some without piano accompaniments.

Part II: Four-part songs for unchanged voices and bass, and a few unison songs for all voices.

Part III: Four-part songs for soprano, alto, tenor, and bass; in addition there are a few songs for basses, to be used as solos or for unison singing, usually with four-part refrain.

Part IV: For two unchanged voices and bass, the bass being optional in some of the numbers; many of the songs comprise melodies which can be sung in unison or as solos.

Part V: Community songs and hymns.

The Laurel Music Reader, in addition to providing material for all types of voice classifications, made a special feature of unison songs. A paragraph from the preface to the book informs us that the predominance of unison songs had purposely been made a feature. "It is in these places that all the singers of all the grades will be enabled to express themselves with a generous degree of musical completeness; also the weak tones of the changing voice will in these unison songs be frequently called into use, and so be greatly strengthened and improved, provided that such tones be rightly produced."

Another book that has been widely used is *Music of Many Lands and Peoples,* edited by Osbourne McConathy, John Beattie, and Russell V. Morgan (New York, Silver Burdett, 1932). The contents of this book show what was considered necessary for mixed classes in the junior high school to carry out the modern theory about the boy's voice. The voice combinations and the number of selections provided for each are as follows:

Bass Solo and Chorus (11)
Boys' Voices, T.T.B.B. (14)
Duets for Sopranos and Altos (13)
Rounds (4)
Songs for Altos (8)
Songs for Alto-Tenors (13)
Songs for Sopranos (18)
Songs for Basses (7)
Sopranos, Altos, and Basses (19)
Sopranos, Altos, Alto-Tenors, Optional Basses (5)
Sopranos, Altos, Alto-Tenors (Optional), and Basses (5)
Sopranos, Altos, Alto-Tenors, Basses (66)
Sopranos, Basses, and Chorus (2)

Soprano Solo and Chorus (9)
Tone Blending Drills (7)
Trios for Sopranos, Mezzo Sopranos, and Altos (2)
Unison (24)

It will be noted that the greater proportion of the numbers is harmonic, for S.A.T.B. or S.A.B., sometimes with optional tenor and sometimes with optional bass. Out of 166 selections, there are eight unison songs for altos, thirteen for alto-tenors, seven for basses, and twenty-four for all voices (boys and girls combined). Of the fourteen selections for boys' voices, nine are of the T.T.B.B. type for the boys' glee clubs, the other numbers being one unison song, one unison with refrain in harmony, one unison with refrain in two parts, and one each for S.A.B. and A.T.B. About thirty numbers are duplications.

The change of attitude towards the boy voice question in school music circles in England is evident from two song books published in the 1930's. One, *A Heritage of Song: A Song Book for Adolescent Boys,* edited and arranged by Robert McLeod, was published in 1932 (London, Curwen; New York, G. Schirmer); the other, the *Clarendon Song Book for Boys with Changing Voices,* edited by W. Gillies Whittaker, Herbert Wiseman, John Wishart, and W. Norman Mellalieu, was published in 1935 (London and New York, Oxford University Press).

The preface to the first book reads: "Within the last ten years or so, a really enlightened inquiry has been going on with regard to the treatment of the voice of the adolescent boy. Experimental courses in voice production and observations of the effect on the mature voice have been made. From these experiments and observations there is no doubt that in schools and colleges, during the years between the ages of fourteen and nineteen, the vocal loss to the country has been enormous. The neglect of the voices during this period has led to an average voice of comparatively standard timbre quite divorced from what nature intended—that is, variety. . . . This collection is intended to develop the *bel canto* of the Italians, the only true foundation of all vocal art. . . . Each song gives a suitable vocal line for the development of the essential resonance at certain pitches. . . . The short part songs also have a specific purpose, and might be called ear-training exercises in tone color, harmonic purpose, and atmosphere."

The McLeod book contains twenty-six unison songs, two three-part songs, and four trios for male voices (tenor, baritone, and bass). Explaining the basis of the selection of unison songs, the editor says of one example: "This, on the face of it, might be merely a song with attractive rhythm and a good obvious chorus. That, however, is not the main purpose of the song—which is to focus the attention on the resonance on and around the tone 'A.' When the appropriate full resonance is found *pianissimo* and persistently used, the voice grows rapidly in power and ease, almost from week to week."

The preface to the *Clarendon Song Book for Boys with Changing Voices* reads: "Not so long ago, a boy, when his voice began to change, was condemned to a merely passive interest in the school music class, and with the young, a passive interest rapidly degenerates into indifference. The boy, therefore, too often acquired the habit of thinking that music was not for him. . . . As a result of carefully recorded experiments and tests which have been carried out for some time in boys' schools of different types, we can say with confidence that we are convinced that the change of voice is seldom a break. It is a gradual and completely natural process of evolution. With due care it is possible and desirable that the boys should sing in class right through this period."[5]

In the *Clarendon Song Book* unison material is used a great deal more than harmonic, and the latter is two- and three-part, never four-part of the soprano, alto, alto-tenor, bass type that is used in American junior high schools.

The shift towards the modern theory in English educational circles is further borne out by the following excerpt on "The Broken Voice," which appeared in an official publication, *Memoranda on Curriculum for Senior Schools: No. VI on Music,* issued in 1933 by the London County Council Schools. "The broken voice, the outstanding problem of the boys' secondary school, will present difficulties in the senior school. But it will be less difficult to deal with the problem if two simple truths are understood and acted on. (*a*) A boy's voice never *breaks.* Physiologically, the vocal chords lengthen at an age varying with individuals, and the voice in consequence changes. Nothing in the vocal apparatus breaks or does anything that could reasonably be described by that word. (*b*) Singing and speaking are the same process, the one being merely a sustained and prolonged form of the other. Every muscle used in one is used in both. During the changing period it is essential they should not be strained; which means that talking and singing (within a restricted force and compass) are both definitely desirable activities. Yet in most cases the boy is left to shout, and the only occasion on which he is not allowed to use his singing voice is in the class, that is, at the one and only time he would be doing it under proper supervision. The best authorities are insistent that quiet and

[5] From the *Clarendon Song Book for Boys with Changing Voices,* copyright 1935 by the Oxford University Press and reprinted by permission. (See also n. 8.)

controlled singing, without too high or too low notes, gives a boy the best chance there is of putting into practice, as a tenor or bass, the lessons he has learnt as a treble."

An interesting piece of evidence comes from an article written in 1940 by G. Kirkham Jones. Mr. Jones was headmaster of a London County Council school and worked with children evacuated from London during World War II: "From a variety of causes, the problem of the change (not the break, if you please) in the voices of the senior boys in our evacuation party is more pressing down here than I ever remember in London. Our lads have grown amazingly, and have matured (at least physically) rapidly in the country. Speaking generally, voices have increased in volume, but I'm afraid, not improved in quality. More than ever, one has to insist on *very* soft singing. The thirteen to fifteen age group, while the smallest section numerically, seems to be the largest vocally, and I'm glad to say, very unwilling to be left out of the singing, nearly all of which, by force of circumstance, is communal. . . . My personal view is that—except in very rare cases where the physical and emotional changes at this puberty period of a boy's life are sudden and violent, and the use of the voice for even reasonable doses of singing and *talking* (please note this inclusion) is likely to lead to permanent definite injury—no boy should be barred altogether from choral singing. . . . It is unwise even to chaff boys with a 'wobble' about the vagaries of their voices—for at this time of life they are hyper-sensitive—or to expose them to the ridicule of their classmates by asking them to give singing, reading, or recitation solos. They can join in choral work of the right kind without being self-conscious. Obviously they must not be allowed to join in ambitious exhibition efforts demanding the utmost purity of tone and accuracy of pitch over a wide vocal range. But school repertoires must be compiled to fit the boys' voices, and not *vice versa,* and must include heaps of simple songs, hymns, and tunes without words, of small tonal range. Uncertainty in voice-placing must be expected, but never commented on; and strain and fatigue must be avoided by the encouragement of very soft singing, humming, or even crooning (of the right sort). Tell the older boys it does not matter if they cannot sing all the notes, high and low—and they must not try to do so. . . . I have my doubts as to the wisdom of attempting part-singing, including *quasi*-tenor and bass, although I must confess I have heard some remarkable results (in exceptionally favorable conditions) at central and secondary schools." [6]

No one in England has a more intimate knowledge about music in the schools of Great Britain than Dr. Cyril Winn, formerly H. M. Staff In-

[6] *Music in Schools* (London), July 1940. (The magazine is now published under the name *Music in Education.*)

spector of Music in Schools, Ministry of Education. For almost a quarter of a century, until he retired a few years ago, the nature of his work enabled him to observe the gradual change of opinion and attitude among school music educators towards the boy voice question. Through the publication of his S.A.B. books, which are now widely used in the schools, Dr. Winn's name has come to be associated with the S.A.B. bass melody type of arrangement.[7] The following statement of his represents the current English viewpoint about the adolescent boy's voice in school music circles: "There is no doubt that in recent years we have officially encouraged singing by adolescent boys (alto, tenor, or bass) while they are still in school, having first consulted Sir James Paget, our leading laryngologist, on the subject, who saw no objection whatever to it."

Asked a few years ago about the extent to which the festival movement provided competition classes in which adolescent boys could participate, Dr. Winn said: "The Competitive Festival movement has done little or nothing to provide classes for adolescent voices, because adjudicators, as a whole, know so little about them. The Non-Competitive Festival, however, which is nowadays the type of festival in which all schools in an area take part, always has groups of adolescents from the secondary schools, singing S.A.B. or S.A.T.B. music. This type of festival has become so popular with the schools that a Schools' Music Association of Great Britain has been formed, and it receives financial backing from the Ministry of Education for administrative purposes. Every three years all these adolescent voices combine to sing some specially composed S.A.T.B. music by such composers as Vaughan Williams, Armstrong Gibbs, and George Dyson, in the Albert Hall, London, under Sir Adrian Boult."

In England there is today quite a demand for material for soprano and baritone, as well as for S.A.B. material of the bass melody type. An example of the first type is *Song Book for Boys,* published in 1955 (Novello). This book contains nineteen unison and ten two-part songs for soprano and baritone. The book is intended to provide for "the problem of the broken voice," by keeping the unison songs within a limited range, and also the two-part songs, where "the second part is printed in the bass clef." Another publication issued in 1955 is *Choral Songs for Voices of Limited Range* (Novello), a collection of nine original compositions by contemporary English composers, three for soprano and baritone, one each for T. Bar. B., T.B.B., and S.B., and three for S.A.B.

[7] Volume I of *The S.A.B. Book* was published in 1932 (London, Boosey and Hawkes); Volume II was published in 1935. These are collections of well known songs arranged by Dr. Winn for three-part singing with the melody in the bass clef. Also prepared by Dr. Winn, and published in recent years, are an S.A.B. collection of old English glees (London, Joseph Williams) and a baritone-bass book for adolescent boys (Leeds, Arnold).

British publishers, however, issue practically no material of the type used for mixed voices and male voices in our junior high schools. The manager of the educational department of one of the leading music houses recently explained the situation to me thus: "While publishers realize that the matter of boys singing through the change of voice in schools is now generally accepted, material for boys with changing voices has never been really a popular field from the publishing point of view. The trouble is that song books in England are published as cheaply as possible, and this means that large sales are essential. It is extremely difficult to bring out books at competitive prices for the smaller field of the adolescent boy. My firm is bringing out shortly two books with soprano and baritone lines for use in boys' and mixed schools, because there appears to be considerable demand for material of this kind."

To get another music educator's point of view, I asked Dr. Herbert Wiseman, formerly Director of Music in the Edinburgh public schools and now head of the Scottish Division of the British Broadcasting Corporation, for a brief statement on the extent and development of the movement to have the boy sing during the change-of-voice period in British schools. He is able to speak from first-hand information as he has adjudicated at competition festivals in many parts of Scotland and England.

At the annual meeting of the British Federation of Music Competition Festivals at Newcastle in 1933, Dr. Wiseman led a discussion on "The Adolescent Boy's Voice," from the point of view of choral singing. This was one of the main topics programmed at the meeting. He based his remarks on a seven-year experiment carried out by W. Norman Mellalieu in the Royal High School for Boys, Edinburgh.[8] A full report of the discussion is given in the 1933 *Year Book* of the federation.

Of the situation as of 1955 Dr. Wiseman states: "Most of the schools in Great Britain have now accepted the principle that boys should sing through adolescence, and also that the voice changes, in most cases, take place gradually and not suddenly. In almost all the secondary schools one now finds mixed voice and male voice choirs. In many competition festivals, classes for such choirs are included in the syllabus. The test pieces are drawn from the current repertory of the choirs, care being taken to ensure that the compass of each part is not excessive." He tells of adjudicating in Hong Kong in April 1955 and hearing about twenty mixed voice and male choirs from schools, several being made up of Chinese boys and girls, singing in English. "So the gospel is spreading all right," he commented.

[8] Mr. Mellalieu describes the plan that was worked out in *The Boy's Changing Voice* (London, Oxford University Press, 1935).

In an article, "Musicians' Miscellany," Dr. Sydney Northcote, another well known adjudicator at English competition festivals, tells of his experience at the Hong Kong Festival in 1954, when he heard about a dozen S.A.T.B. choirs of students between the ages of fifteen and nineteen, composed of the equivalent of English high school girls and grammar school boys, almost all Chinese-speaking, yet singing most effectively in English. "The freshness and buoyancy of these youthful choirs was truly exhilarating," he remarks. As to the increasing amount of S.A.B. material being used in England, his opinion is that while it is an admirable compromise, the idea of giving the melody to the baritone or bass, with added parts above, should not be pushed too far or too long, because the male voices will not learn the *feel* of their normal place in the structure. He also makes the following interesting comment: "We know that for the last twenty or thirty years the moment of change in the boy's voice has tended to become progressively earlier. It is certain that little is gained by trying to preserve the treble voice very much longer than nature intends." [9]

In Canada, a fairly accurate picture of the school music program can be gained by examining the syllabuses of the provincial competition festivals. One of the main features of these festivals is the choral competitions for schools. The festival movement is very closely linked up with the schools in that it offers competition classes for every level of the school music program for which there is a demand. However, classes in which adolescent boys can participate are very few in any of the provincial festivals, even though in such cities as Winnipeg and Vancouver where the largest festivals are held, many schools follow the modern theory about the boy's voice. In Ontario, the provincial festival did not prove to be the success it was in western Canada, so it was abandoned during World War II, but the county school festival has taken its place under the sponsorship of the Ontario Department of Education, and has been very rewarding.

"School music in Ontario has been influenced by the educational systems of both England and the United States of America. . . . Leaders in music education in this province have tried to combine the thoroughness and artistry of English standards with the enthusiasm and organizing genius of our neighbours to the south," says Dr. G. Roy Fenwick, formerly Supervisor of Music, Hamilton, Ontario, and now Director of Music, On-

[9] *Music Education* (London), March-April, 1955. For further comments on time of voice maturation see Chapter 3.

tario Department of Education, in his book, *The Function of Music Education* (Toronto, W. J. Gage, 1951).[10]

In 1941 a bulletin, *Training the Voices of Children and Adolescents,* was issued by the authority of the Ontario Minister of Education. Under the heading, "The Adolescent Voice—Boys," the official attitude towards the boy voice question is given as follows: "During adolescence the boy's voice deepens in pitch and quality, due to the rapid growth of the vocal cords. The voice 'changes' but does not 'break,' unless a great strain is placed upon it. Boys do not cease to speak during adolescence, and except in rare cases, need not cease to sing. . . . It is imperative that boys' voices be properly classified, that they sing within their easy range, and that the tone be not forced. While unison songs may be still used, provided they are transposed to suit the compass of the voices, teachers are urged to develop part-singing. In this way only, will the boys feel that they have an important place in the singing period. Fortunately, song material is now available which is suitable both in vocal arrangement and text. . . . The generally accepted theory is that, if properly produced, the boy's voice gradually descends . . . passing through the approximate ranges of alto, tenor, and bass, before definitely settling into the man's voice." "Boy tenor" is used for the third part, though "alto-tenor" is used to some extent by those who are familiar with American publications.

In 1945, a book in line with the spirit of the bulletin was published in Toronto: *Youthful Voices,* by Don Wright, Director of Music, London, Ontario, in cooperation with a group of ten Ontario supervisors and the Provincial Supervisor of Music (Gordon V. Thompson). The approximate ranges of the tenor and bass parts are given as, A to F', and $B_{,}$ to A (bass staff).

Dr. Fenwick has very kindly provided for this chapter the following statement on the situation in Ontario as of 1955: "Music educators in Ontario are nearly all convinced that boys should continue to sing during the voice-changing period, and the idea of the no-break theory has been generally accepted. Most of the school festivals today have classes for S.A.T.B. In all graded schools and a large number of ungraded rural schools, songs are being used in four-part arrangements. This has had a marked effect upon the attitude of the boys, who now feel they are needed instead of being a nuisance. The singing has improved greatly and the attitude of the entire school has become much more enthusiastic."

[10] The book deals with the history of school music in Ontario from its first recognition as a part of public education in 1847, when a music teacher was appointed at the Toronto Normal School. One chapter is devoted to the festival movement in the Ontario schools, with discussions of both the competitive and non-competitive types of festival.

Dr. Will Earhart, after a visit to London in 1935, made some observations on the difference of emphasis that is placed on the type of material used in English schools which carry out the modern theory regarding the boy's voice: "The United States long ago settled the question of the boy singing throughout the mutation period in the affirmative—by preparing special parts of carefully restricted range. On the question of voice, the English are right for them, and wrong for us. They like hearty free expression and use more unison and less harmonic work than we do; and to keep a boy singing their way would be impossible rather than unwise for us. One sees this in their school music literature as compared with ours. I had a long talk about this with a very musical headmaster of a London school that had consistently won prizes at the London school competitions. We came to the conclusion that the difference in emphasis between melodic and harmonic aspects accounted for much. For educational purposes, I think that the continued singing during the adolescent period on modest inner parts of restricted range is the more promising way of considering the boy's voice. Hence I am on the American side of the boy voice question."

In saying that the English "like hearty free expression," Dr. Earhart is referring to the kind of tone he heard in the elementary schools (schools with eight grades). A good description of the kind of tone was given by the London County Council Schools in 1933: "It is nowadays no uncommon thing to hear in the schools, even in the poorest districts, tone which for both purity and volume, was a generation ago the exclusive prerogative of the cathedral choir" (*Memoranda on Curriculum for Senior Schools: No. VI on Music*).

Tone of the big hearty type can be heard in the United States in such Episcopal churches as St. Thomas', New York, and the Cathedral of St. John the Divine, New York. It is possible to develop it in seventh and eighth grade school boys whose voices have not started to lower, but soon will; it is not possible in younger boys, for their voices have not matured sufficiently to produce it. In contrast with this type of tone is the so-called "floating" type, which is considered best for our elementary school working conditions up to and through the sixth grade; it is light in character and volume. With junior high school boys it is, of course, fuller, for the boys are older and the voices more developed; but it is different from the hearty type, and it is not so intensive.

Just as the "hearty free" tone is heard at its best from seventh and eighth grade boys in English schools, so the "floating" tone is heard at its best in a junior high school boys' choir of unchanged voices. The junior high school choir that would compare with an English school choir of the caliber that takes part in competitions is able to sing three-part (S.S.A.) music, whereas the English choir would not attempt more than two-part (S.A.), because of the difficulty in obtaining an alto section for three-part music. The way in which the English voices have been used is not conducive to building an alto section; the American way is.

Today there is hardly a high school in America that does not have its mixed choral organization, in which a good bass section will always be found, and in which the tenor section (made up of alto-tenors and tenors, albeit tonally immature in comparison with the tenor section of an adult organization) can always be relied on to make itself heard in a satisfactory manner provided that the music does not call for strenuous singing, and provided that the tenor part is within the comfortable range of the section. This is evidence that the type of training the boy receives in the junior high school by the prevailing alto-tenor plan has no injurious effect on the development of the boy's future voice, but rather the opposite, judging by the caliber of the singing heard today by the choral organizations of the high school.

· 2 ·

The Evolution of the Alto-Tenor Plan

To anyone engaged in public school music in the United States the term "alto-tenor" needs no explanation, but to a musician who comes across the word for the first time, its meaning is somewhat of a puzzle. Even in America where the alto-tenor plan is followed, the term has not yet attained the distinction of being included in any dictionary—musical or otherwise—as far as I know. In England neither the term nor the plan it describes is used, in spite of the fact that in recent years a movement to have the boy sing during the adolescent period has been growing. Percy A. Scholes did not mention it in his article on "Voice" in the *Oxford Companion to Music,* in either the first or second edition, although he devoted some attention to the question of the boy singing during puberty, mentioning Edinburgh and Winnipeg (but not the United States) as places where the experiment has been tried. When his attention was drawn to the omission, he asked what the term meant and requested a short article about it to include in a later edition of the book. The article appears in the Appendix to the third and fourth British editions (1939 and 1941).

"Alto-tenor" is the term used to describe and classify the boy's voice after it has lowered to the stage when the changed voice begins to develop. It was coined as the result of the need for a suitable designation for the third part of four-part voice music for adolescent boys in the upper grades of the elementary school, in the days before the junior high school. The term was applied not only to the voice but also to the part. The voice is still alto, but it has lowered to the extent that the boy can sing in the tenor range; the quality, however, has not yet become masculine, that is, either tenor or bass.

The range G below middle C to G an octave above has come to be the accepted alto-tenor range. Many years of experiment in the schools have proved that this is the safest and most practical one for carrying out the alto-tenor idea of voice classification. This range is the comfortable one for alto-tenors as a general class, although some are able to sing several notes higher than the high G, while others can sing a few notes lower than the low G. The criterion for determining that the alto-tenor stage has been reached is the ability to sing low F, together with the development of a timbre peculiarly associated with the changing voice when it has reached this stage.

Every boy's voice passes through the alto-tenor stage, in most cases during the junior high school years. A few boys, however, reach the alto-tenor stage in the sixth grade, while some whose voices are changing very slowly do not reach it until they are in the high school. "Alto-tenor" (the voice and the classification) is, therefore, associated particularly with the junior high school period. Either because their voices change to bass quickly, or because their voices pass through the alto-tenor stage during the summer vacation, some boys skip the classification altogether.

It is worth noting that although the term alto-tenor has come to be generally accepted, two well-known authorities on the adolescent boy's voice, Thaddeus P. Giddings, for many years Director of Music, Minneapolis Schools, and Hollis Dann, author of many music textbooks for schools and founder of the National High School Chorus, never recognized it—in spite of the fact that they carried out in their work the principles of the alto-tenor plan. Mr. Giddings considered the term misleading, saying there was no such voice. His argument was that a boy's voice was either alto or tenor, even though an alto might also be able to sing the tenor part and a tenor the alto part. Dr. Dann did not use the term; instead he spoke of the "boy tenor" whose range was E or F (below middle C) to A or B (above middle C). "This is distinctly the tenor compass, therefore the voice is called 'boy tenor,' " he says. "The compass of the boy alto and the boy tenor is indefinite, the compass of the same voice varying widely at different times, as does the length of time the boy can comfortably sing alto and tenor parts." Speaking of the "remarkable uniformity" of compass at the boy-bass stage, he remarks: "Nearly all adolescent boys have this limited compass and boy-bass quality regardless of whether the voice eventually develops into a tenor or a bass. During this period, lasting approximately two years, more or less, there is usually no definite indication of the future classification of the voice." [1]

Investigating the origin of the word "alto-tenor" and how the alto-tenor idea was evolved, I was surprised to find that such pioneers of public school music as Edward Birge, Will Earhart, Charles Farnsworth, Osbourne McConathy, and others, could give no information. Ralph Baldwin,

[1] Hollis Dann, *Conductor's Book,* Hollis Dann Song Series (New York, American Book, 1936).

then Director of Music, Public Schools, Hartford, Connecticut, supplied the following: "I would not dare to say where the word originated, or who was the first person to use it. I began teaching public school music in Northampton, Massachusetts, in 1899. As soon as one of the schools was ready for part music, I put the boys with changing voices on the third part, the tenor part. These boys were called tenors. However, outside of school, in speaking of these voices or of the part they sang, I called the voice and the part 'alto-tenor' so that it would not be confused with the mature tenor."

Eldridge W. Newton, for many years music editor for Ginn and Company, thought the term was first used about 1894: "The term referred to a part which might be sung by a girl alto or by an incipient boy tenor. I remember distinctly my first summer school for music supervisors in Boston in 1893. Luther Whiting Mason, George James M. McLaughlin, then his assistant in the Boston schools, and George Veazie, then Director of Music in Chelsea, Massachusetts, were there. All three used the term 'alto-tenor' in conversation, but in writing they used the term 'boy alto,' as you will find in the Preface of Mason and Veazie's book, published by Ginn and Company, Boston, in 1891." The book referred to is *The New Fourth Reader* of the National Music Course Series. The subtitle indicated that the book was designed to meet the peculiar needs in the upper grades of boys' and mixed schools. The introductory chapter states: "All boys with changed voices should read from the bass staff, and every boy alto from the middle or alto staff. . . . A close watch should be kept upon the boy altos, as many possess voices nearing the transition stage, who, as soon as the voice settles below the requirements of the alto part and gives evidence of the transition period, should be transferred to the bass section where they can read from the bass staff such notes as are within their limits.

"The music is mostly in three-part composition, but it is arranged in four-part form upon three staves; the upper staff has the first soprano and the second soprano parts, the middle staff the alto part, and the lowest staff the bass clef, the part thereon being merely a doubling of the alto part with occasional exceptions." The exceptions are that four-part harmony is often used as cadences, and at the end of the book there are a few pages of four-part compositions. The ranges of the voice classifications are given as follows:

Nowhere in the book is there any mention of the term "alto-tenor," but evidence that the idea of the alto-tenor had been crystallizing is to be found in an earlier school music textbook, *The Third Reader for Mixed Voices,* from a series, The Normal Course, edited by John W. Tufts (New York, Silver Burdett, 1885). In this book there are a few examples of four-part music in three-part harmony, similar to the examples in the Mason and Veazie book, the range of the alto part being the same as in the latter book. This, as far as I have been able to discover, is the first school text to apply the rudiments of the alto-tenor idea.

The earliest published music in which the word alto-tenor appears seems to be the *Beacon Song Collection,* edited by Herbert Griggs (New York, Silver Burdett, 1895). In this collection most of the music is in four-part harmony. Mr. Griggs had the reputation of being an excellent teacher and was considered a vital force in public school music. His work as an editor, however, is rather inconsistent, for his third part (the tenor) is indicated variously as "tenor-alto," "tenor or alto," and "alto-tenor," these words being printed in the score, while some compositions are marked in the orthodox manner, S.A.T.B. The range of the third part all through the book keeps fairly consistently within the accepted range of today, $G_{,}$ to G (treble clef).

Of the music published for school use in the early days of school music, Edward Birge, in his *History of Public School Music in the United States* (rev. ed., New York, Oliver Ditson, 1937), says: "The music supervisor had little guide except the printed suggestions in the music books, supplemented by his own pedagogical ability. He thus became more or less a law to himself, a condition highly favorable for developing initiative, and out of this grew a characteristic feature of the period, namely, the editing and publishing of a large number of school music readers." A sample of this initiative, an arrangement by Leo R. Lewis, Tufts College, from the Beacon Series No. 161 (Silver Burdett, 1901), is reprinted on page 23.

Knowing that Professor Lewis had an extensive library of materials used during the beginnings of school music in America, I consulted him some years ago on the source of the alto-tenor idea, and the place and date of the first use of the plan. As to the meaning of the notation "Tenor and Alto" for the third part, he explained: "The term 'alto-tenor' was not used for this part, as the tenors and the altos read from notes as they are accustomed to see them. Girl altos never have occasion to become familiar with the tenor notation, but boy altos by using such editions, have before them notes placed as they will later read them, if they turn out to be tenors. Under timely guidance of their teachers, they shift their reading to the upper notes and are thus trained, as to their eyes, for singing

GREAT AND MARVELLOUS ARE THY WORKS.

From A. R. Gaul's "Holy City."
Arranged by Leo R. Lewis.

Copyright, 1901, by Silver, Burdett & Company.

from standard editions the tenor part. Many octavo compositions and several music books were issued with this double notation by various publishers. Soon the term 'alto-tenor' was prefixed to the part and the two-note notation ceased to appear."

Asked to comment on his reason for introducing the two-note idea, Professor Lewis said: "By the late nineties four-part singing had been sufficiently developed in some high schools of the larger cities in the eastern states of America to permit oratorio and cantata performances, the singers using standard published editions. There were protests, often causing rather acrimonious discussion, against the forcing of young tenors and basses, and it cannot be doubted that there were cases of permanent singing disability resulting from the practice. As against this occasional disadvantage, there was the argument of cultural training of the participants. With the obvious intention of meeting the situation, educationally as well as vocally, there came into existence a plan of presenting the tenor part as an adult reads it, on the same staff with the same part as an unchanged voice reads it. The first embodiment of this plan is found in the Beacon Series No. 161."

With the advent of the junior high school movement at the beginning of the century, it became possible to experiment with the plan on a large scale and bring about its general use in America. The plan proved itself beneficial to the boy's future voice, not injurious to it. Hence, it can be said that the junior high school has been the proving ground for the acceptance of the modern theory about the boy's changing voice as opposed to the traditional theory.

· 3 ·

The Boy's Voice During Adolescence

The success that is possible with boys' changing voices during the adolescent period depends a good deal on the way the voices have been used in preadolescence. If a boy has been trained to use his singing and his speaking voice correctly before adolescence sets in, he has formed good habits of voice production. He automatically uses his vocal mechanism properly, and so, while his voice is changing, he is able to sing without any trouble other than that which occurs as the result of the workings of nature during the mutation. Consequently, it behooves a junior high school teacher to find out how the voices of the boys entering the seventh grade classes have been used in the grade schools.

THE CHEST VOICE

Downward vocalization is the best method of training boys with unchanged voices to form good habits of voice production.[1] Downward vocalization exercises prevent the use of the chest voice. Singing with the chest voice means that the mechanism is not being used correctly, and the more the chest voice is used during preadolescence, the more problems the boy will have with his voice during the adolescent period, especially when it is going through the transition stage.

It would be difficult to find a preadolescent boy, even a highly trained choirboy, who had never used his chest voice. Although the choirboy who has been under good care from an early age may never have used it in *singing,* it is most unlikely that he has never used it in *speaking*. The American boy, because of the nature of his games, indulges in a good deal of shouting. But if the voice work done in the classroom has been such that he has formed good habits, he will be less apt to use his chest voice when at play; he may find he can make the necessary noise without having to shout.

[1] This matter is fully treated in William J. Finn's *The Art of the Choral Conductor* (Boston, Birchard, 1939).

An occasional shout is not in itself bad. For one thing, it is a means of letting off steam; and as the boy grows older, he needs outlets for the new energy he acquires as a result of his general growth. A shout is sometimes beneficial provided the voice is used correctly, and for some special purpose. For example, in singing, a shout under control, tempered down to a sustained tone on a definite pitch, can be used to develop a more intensive *forte*. But this exercise is recommended only occasionally in a rehearsal, and then only for a few seconds at a time. If it is used too frequently and kept up for too long a time, the voice is subjected to strain. A boy soon realizes this, for his voice begins to feel sore.

In any singing a boy does outside the classroom, it is probable that he uses his chest voice mainly, especially if the singing is of the community type in which volume rather than quality is expected. However, the amount of such singing that he does is negligible, comparatively speaking, and if a teacher is on the alert in the classroom, chest tone need never be heard there.

SPEECH TRAINING

It is natural that as the voice becomes more powerful during adolescence, the boy begins to feel a new vocal consciousness. He likes not only to yell but also to make all sorts of queer sounds, often by way of mimicry. There seems to be no sound that he cannot imitate. Unfortunately, in yelling and making these sounds, he can, and very often does, begin to develop bad habits which are reflected in his speech and singing. The tone quality is raucous; the vowels lack resonance and lose their individual color; enunciation is indistinct; speech becomes slovenly and lacks the naïve inflection of the younger boy. The adolescent may even develop an affected way of talking, perhaps in imitation of someone older than himself. The more these faults become habits, the more they hinder the natural development of the future voice. Unfortunately, beyond telling the boy to speak out, little attention seems to be paid in the classroom to helping him cultivate a pleasant speaking voice. Therefore, he speaks loudly, and in doing so, he forces, using chest voice production. If, instead, the boy were asked to speak clearly, he would be more likely to use his voice correctly.

Although a critical attitude towards speech should be developed in the classroom, the teacher should bear in mind that good speech habits are not instilled by artificial means. These only make a boy self-conscious, and self-consciousness is fatal to correct use of the voice. Instead, if the boy can be interested in what he is doing, the conditions are likely to be favorable for clear speech and hence correct use of the voice. Devices can, and at times must, be used, but they should be used subtly. If speech training receives attention during preadolescence, faults are not so likely to develop. If they do, they can be cured more readily. Although there is little time in the junior high school music lesson for individual or group reading of the words of the music, some concentration on reading the words will help to focus the boy's attention on good speech, and this, in turn, will have a good effect on the singing. The singing will be tonally better to the degree that the diction is better.

In her book *Speech Training in the Schools* (London, Evans Bros., 1929), Marjorie Gullan gives a series of lessons for dealing with the main faults of speech. By adaptation, these lessons may be applied to students of various ages. The following faults are listed: (*1*) poor quality and quantity of tone; (*2*) misshapen and badly pronounced vowels; (*3*) thick, muffled utterances; (*4*) lack of muscular activity of lips, tongue, and jaw. Miss Gullan says in her introduction that "these lessons must be given in the spirit of a game which all play together . . . the pupils should look upon their speech training as a delightful and absorbing game which is never associated with drudgery or unwilling effort. In the school curriculum, we have only a few minutes here and there to devote to this most necessary subject, and therefore we must obtain the utmost concentration when practicing, if we are to achieve good results."

THE LOWERING PROCESS

Of all the observable signs associated with adolescence, the speaking voice is the most reliable in estimating the status of the singing voice of the boy at any time during the adolescent period. As the speaking voice lowers, so does the singing voice, but the former always lowers first. The first sign of adolescence in the speaking voice is the change in tone quality; it becomes fuller and deeper, and it may sound husky. Some voices waver in pitch after a while, and this is often a source of embarrassment to the boy. He becomes annoyed because he can do nothing about it, the muscles of the larynx not yet having developed sufficiently to control the voice. The uncertainty of pitch may persist until the changed voice has developed somewhat, but disappears as the voice matures. If the voice is a slowly changing one, only the change in tone quality is noticeable. Wavering in pitch is not likely to occur.

As adolescence progresses, the boy finds that he can sing a few notes lower and that as the new notes develop, the highest notes of his range become difficult to sing. Then, as a few more new notes develop, these highest notes disappear. In other words, the voice gradually lowers as a whole. This lowering process, which is one of the chief characteristics of adolescence, continues throughout the adolescent period until the changed voice emerges and develops to its "settled" status.

Up to a certain stage, the lowering voice is still the boy voice, an unchanged but changing one. It lowers through the second soprano to the alto stage. As the voice continues to lower, it develops to the "youth" stage; the voice sounds neither like a boy's nor like a man's, but has a quality peculiar to this stage. When the speaking voice reaches this stage, the singing voice is at the late alto stage, and the quality of the speaking voice serves as a guide that it will soon be time to classify the boy as alto-tenor. Once the changed speaking voice has developed, the changed singing voice can be expected. As the changed voice develops and new notes emerge in the lower range, the boy voice gradually disappears until little of it remains. The voice is now at the stage when it can be classified as tenor or bass. The change will occur more rapidly if the voice is destined to be bass than if it is to be tenor.

When the lowering reaches its limits, the lowering process becomes, as it were, a moving-up one; the boy loses some of the lowest notes he has been able to sing. The disappearance of the lowest notes is compensated by an extension of the upper range of the changed voice. Once the moving-up process stops, the voice is said to have "settled"; that is, the range becomes stationary. Not until the voice has settled should a boy's classification be considered his final one, the one he will have as an adult.

Because of the moving-up of the range, some boys first classified as Bass II have to be reclassified as Bass I, and others first classified as Bass I have to be reclassified as Tenor II. Some of the latter may become high baritones, able to sing in the Tenor II range. If so, as their voices mature, timbre determines whether they should be considered high baritones or Tenor II.

Once a voice has settled, its range can be extended only by training. W. S. Drew believes that "partly as a result of healthy exercise, and partly in connection with the inevitable process of growing up, for the large majority of singers the *tessitura* not only increases its range as the voice becomes more trained and flexible but also moves up bodily, with the result that passages which are difficult at the age of twenty-five become easy to sing at the age of thirty. This is especially true of English voices, which develop slowly and require delicate treatment in the early stages." [2] This moving-up refers, of course, to the settled voice and not to the unsettled changed voice.

Many conductors of high school and college choral organizations in the United States are of the opinion that the settled voices of American young men move up at an earlier age than that given by Drew for English

[2] From *Singing: The Art and Craft,* copyright 1937 by the Oxford University Press, London, and reprinted by permission.

voices: around twenty for basses and a year or two later for tenors. This may be due to the fact that English boys do not sing during adolescence (because of tradition), and consequently their adult voice development is later than that of American boys who have sung during this period. That the voices of American boys settle at an earlier age may in some cases be a result of nationality, since children of continental European nationality and parentage, especially of the Low Countries, seem to show an earlier maturity than the English; in other cases the earlier settling may have to do with the climatic conditions and the geographic location of the boys' homes. In places with an all-the-year-round warm climate like that of Los Angeles and places of high altitude like Salt Lake City the boys' voices in high school choirs sound more mature than those in eastern high school choirs.[3]

THE DIFFERENT STAGES OF THE CHANGING VOICE

The different stages through which the boy's voice passes during the adolescent period are, according to the classification of the alto-tenor plan, Soprano II, Alto, Alto-Tenor, Tenor or Bass. Some boys pass from Alto-Tenor to Tenor and then to Bass. When this happens, the boy does not remain long in the tenor classification.

Range rather than timbre determines the classification of the changing voice, but timbre rather than range is the determining factor when the changed voice has developed considerably. Generally speaking, while

[3] The process of voice maturation seems to start earlier in California than it does in the eastern states. In southern California, especially, the tone of the boys' voices in junior and senior high school choirs is more mature than one expects. Is this due to the effect of the climate? Of course, it may be due in part to the type of training or to the nationalities of some of the boys, particularly those of European parentage (for a full-blooded tone is characteristic of the speaking and singing of southern Europeans). Having heard several Los Angeles high school choirs, and attended a demonstration of musical activities of the Los Angeles schools, I had a talk with Mr. Louis Woodson Curtis, at the time Director of Music, about the matter. He said there was evidence that the boy's voice matures more quickly in California than it does in other parts of the country; that his suspicion of this possibility was aroused when he discovered that the alto-tenor parts of the school music books prepared by eastern editors were too high for the alto-tenors in Los Angeles junior high schools; that this might be expected and regarded as normal in those schools where there was a decided Latin parentage (there being large Mexican and Italian colonies in Los Angeles), but was also noticeable where the population was definitely American. Dr. Will Earhart, formerly Director of Music, Pittsburgh, after a stay of a year in California, was of the same opinion. General growth does not always include development of vocal organ, he said; but while the degree of change of voice is not precisely correlated with the degree of physical development, some degree of change of voice is almost invariably associated with evident rapid development. The matter is one that is worth investigating, for there is little information about it other than the opinions of individual teachers who have had experience with adolescent voices in different kinds of climates.

timbre indicates whether the unsettled changed voice is likely to develop into tenor or bass, both range and timbre have to be taken into account, range being the more important factor at first.

The ranges of the adolescent boy's voice up to the stage that it changes, as given below, are the generally accepted ones. Not all boy sopranos (Soprano I) can sing high G, however; for many the limit is high F. The well-trained boy has the wider range. Some altos can sing higher than C (octave above middle C), but as they have little opportunity in the music used in school, these notes tend to disappear. The alto-tenor whose voice is changing slowly can usually sing higher than G or A; if he can sing higher than A, the voice may be developing into tenor.

Ranges of the Adolescent Boy's Voice

Soprano II. When a boy is classified as second soprano because of the signs of adolescence in his speaking voice, he is still able to sing first soprano. Although comfortable range determines a boy's classification, at this stage other factors may have to be taken into consideration, for example age or physical development, both of which may be in advance of the voice status. An older boy or one of more than average physique will be happier classified as second soprano for psychological reasons even though he is a first soprano; furthermore, the voice is encouraged to lower. Any difficulty about high E or F indicates that the voice has reached the second soprano stage.

Just before adolescence sets in, the tone of the older boy soprano takes on a peculiarly beautiful quality, one quite different from that of a younger boy soprano. It is fuller and has a richness it did not have before, the highest notes having a brilliancy heard only in the older boy soprano voice. This tone quality, when heard in a soprano section, indicates that some of the boys have reached the adolescent stage vocally. In a choir of well-trained voices it is very noticeable, but it can also be heard among untrained voices.

Alto. As the voice lowers, difficulty with the highest notes of the second soprano range indicates that the boy should be transferred to alto. If there is no difficulty—and sometimes there seems to be none, not only in voices which are changing slowly but also in the better than average voices which are changing quickly—the appearance of new low notes in the lower range serves as the sign to change the boy's classification. When first classified as alto, he can still sing second soprano for some time, and he is possibly more effective as a second soprano, but because the voice is lowering, he soon finds it more comfortable singing alto. The tone quality is deeper and fuller than before. It approximates that of the female adult contralto if the boy has been well trained, except that it lacks the depth of the contralto voice. The real boy alto voice is a rarity. In the untrained voice the tone may be raucous if the boy has got into the habit of using chest voice production. A boy will remain in the alto classification from a few months up to about a year if the voice is developing to bass, and a year or longer if the voice is developing to tenor.

Alto-Tenor. While the boy is in the alto classification, his speaking voice has been lowering to the "youth" stage. When it reaches this stage, it is time to classify him as alto-tenor. The lowering is easier to observe now than before. A rapid or sudden lowering indicates that the voice is changing to bass, and a slow lowering that it is likely to change to tenor. The tone quality has a timbre that is peculiar to the voice at the alto-tenor stage, being more effective in the upper range at first, and in the lower later on.

There are many variations in the length of time a boy can remain in the alto-tenor classification because of the varying rates of the changing process in the individual voices. The boy who becomes bass and who does not skip the classification may be alto-tenor from a few months to a semester or longer, but generally less than a year. Some skip the classification because their voices go through the transition during the long vacation. In the case of the voice that becomes tenor, the change from the alto-tenor to the tenor status is very gradual, taking from a year to eighteen months and even longer, and it is difficult to detect.

Tenor. Since the tenor voice develops so gradually and imperceptibly that it is hard to observe that any change is taking place, it is not possible to say exactly when an alto-tenor becomes tenor. The voice is called tenor when it has lowered to the tenor range—to C (octave below middle C)—even though it shows little or no tenor timbre. It is because the tenor voice takes so long to develop that tenors are extremely rare in the junior high school and their voices immature in the high school. And because of the immaturity, the voices of high school tenors must be used with great care, especially in the upper range, until they have developed sufficiently to be used like adult voices. This means that the music chosen must not demand strenuous singing or too high a *tessitura.*

Two types of tenor voices are found in the high school: those with an alto-tenor timbre and those without this timbre. The tone quality of the former lacks any trace of adult timbre and the speaking voice shows the same lack, but as the voice matures, the alto-tenor character disappears. The difference between this voice and the alto-tenor is that the former has a longer lower range. The second type of tenor is the more common. The voice has an adult timbre to an extent. Three categories are found: (*1*) the tenor who can pass into the falsetto easily around high E or F with no perceptible change of voice and can then sing to A (second space, treble clef) or higher; (*2*) the tenor who eventually becomes the average tenor as an adult and whose range in high school is C (second space, bass clef) to high F (bass clef)—included in this category is the voice that may have to be classified as Bass I for a time; (*3*) the tenor who, as his voice develops, becomes a high baritone. This voice can easily be wrongly classified, for the boy is able to sing high F or G with ease.

Bass. With the first sign of the changed speaking voice while the boy is in the alto-tenor classification, indicating that the changed voice is developing, he should be classified as bass sooner rather than later, even if he can sing only a few notes in the changed voice. The highest notes of the alto-tenor range will now disappear more or less quickly, but the lower ones will remain. However, the boy will not be able to sing the lowest notes in his unchanged voice; he will sing them in his changed voice. The policy should be to encourage the changed voice to develop, no matter how much of the unchanged voice remains in the lower alto-tenor range. The real boy bass is as rare as the real adult bass. The majority of boy basses are baritones, low, medium, and high. The adolescent bass voice has the same tonal character as the adult bass except that it lacks maturity. This develops rather quickly, however, so that the tone of a junior high school bass section sounds quite bass-like and that of a high school section almost as mature as that of an adult amateur group, especially if the voices are selected. Considerable differences are found in the comfortable ranges of boy basses during the junior high school period, but by the time the boy gets to high school the voice is nearing the settled stage. This is likely to occur in the eleventh or twelfth year of school. The approximate ranges are given below.

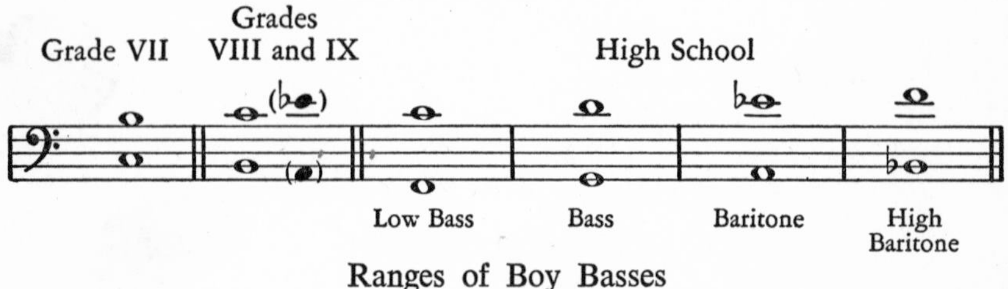

Ranges of Boy Basses

It is characteristic of the boy bass whose voice has developed considerably that he can sing a few notes lower than he will be able to when his voice has settled. As long as he sings in a range that is comfortable, there is no harm in his singing the very lowest notes he can produce. An occasional boy bass will be able to sing the highest notes with ease, sometimes to high F or G. If he were to sing the lower scale of F or G only, he would be classified as bass, and if he were to sing the upper scale only, he might be classified as tenor. The problem is how to classify him. The safe plan is to put him in the lower classification and retest him later.

· 4 ·

The Comfortable Range Policy

The foundation of any successful plan to preserve the boy's singing voice during adolescence is the "comfortable range" policy. As the alto-tenor plan, for example, is carried out in the junior high school, a boy is transferred to the next lower classification as soon as he begins to have difficulty with the highest notes of the one he is in. Thus the lowest notes have an opportunity to develop, while the highest notes, being unused, gradually disappear. Success with the alto-tenor plan lies in encouraging the voice to lower, for that is what nature intends it to do. Accordingly, when there is any doubt about the classification of a voice during the adolescent period, it is best to put the boy in the lower one, with the proviso that he must never force the lowest notes. If he is taught to realize the importance of singing only in his comfortable range, he will never need to force, and with the music that is today available to suit all the voice conditions in the junior high school, forcing is uncalled for.

Obviously the "comfortable range" lies within the full range. A boy's full range should therefore be noted at each voice test, for the change between tests reveals the rate at which the voice is changing (lowering in pitch). If the rate is slow, the full range may be more or less stationary for a time, possibly for more than a semester, but less than a year; if the rate is more rapid, the full range is likely to alter during a semester. On the other hand, the comfortable range of the changing voice at any stage remains about the same for a time: generally speaking, a semester for quickly changing voices, and a year or longer for slowly changing ones. This comparative stability of the comfortable range makes it possible to classify boys' voices according to the alto-tenor plan and carry out the type of choral program that exists today in the junior high school.

FLEXIBILITY OF CLASSIFICATION

A certain amount of flexibility in classifying changing voices is possible; that is to say, a boy may be put temporarily in the classification above or below the one he is in. It depends on his comfortable range at the time. Thus, a boy classified as a second soprano may be temporarily classified as a first soprano, or as an alto; or a boy classified as an alto may be temporarily classified as a second soprano, or as an alto-tenor. This flexibility of classification is possible when the ranges of the two classifications overlap and the boy has a comfortable range that covers the ranges of both: if, for instance, when classified as second soprano he can comfortably sing the first soprano part, or as second soprano he can comfortably sing the alto part; and similarly when as alto he is assigned to second soprano, or to alto-tenor. The teacher should take advantage of this flexibility only as occasion demands, to get a better balance of parts or to bolster up a weak section.

If a voice is changing quickly and if the speaking voice shows that the transition to the changed status has started, it is not advisable to have an alto-tenor sing alto, even if he can, because of the policy of encouraging the boy to find his changed voice.[1] If the voice is changing slowly, however, there is no reason why an alto-tenor should not sing alto when necessary, provided the part is comfortable for him.

NONPERMANENCY OF CLASSIFICATION

The voice classification within a group of boys with changing voices cannot be considered final for any given period because each voice changes at its own rate. Nevertheless, a section of a group of boys can remain more or less in one classification for a semester or the greater part of a semester. The flexibility already mentioned helps to make this possible. The essential thing is that a boy should not stay in a classification once he feels uncomfortable in it. In a glee club, where permanency of classification is necessary for, say, a concert or a contest, the selection of voices at the beginning of the semester should be such that they will have developed to the extent necessary for singing the different parts with ease towards the date of the concert or contest.

THE HIGH NOTE DIFFICULTY IN THE CHANGED VOICE

Because of the new tonal power the boy feels in his changed voice, he is tempted to force the highest notes of his range before they have developed sufficiently so that he can sing them with ease. If he forces them, throatiness results. It is usually the boy with a promising voice

[1] This is the point on which the alto-tenor and the counter-tenor plans differ in policy. In the latter plan the boy whose voice has reached the transition stage is encouraged to keep his unchanged voice in action and sing as an alto, even though he may sing tenor and bass leads informally at rehearsals, because he wants to.

who wants to sing high notes before they have developed. Hence the teacher should keep an ear on the young bass in the junior high school and on the young tenor in the high school at any passages in choral music that call for the highest notes of the range.

A psychological factor may affect a boy's use of the high notes of his immature changed voice. When he has difficulty singing them, he becomes dissatisfied with his voice. If he is a bass, he may want to stop singing altogether; if he is a tenor, he may want to sing bass under the impression that his voice is not suited for the tenor part. The young bass and the young tenor must be enlightened as to how the notes of the upper range develop.

A tenor whose voice shows signs of promise is often lost to the tenor section during the high school years if he is allowed to assume a wrong attitude about high notes. He wants to be a tenor; his instincts tell him he will be a tenor; but he gets impatient at the slow development of his voice. He worries if the highest notes of the range do not develop, and he worries if he has to be classified as bass. Many tenors, although they may not be lost in the long run, are not as good tenors as nature intended them to be because they are not aware of the way in which the tenor voice develops and matures.

In the high school some boys are classified first as tenor, then as bass, and finally as tenor. A boy is classified as bass because he is not comfortable singing the tenor part. After singing bass for a time, he finds he is not comfortable singing a bass part. He may report this, but whether he does or not, the timbre of his voice should be particularly noted at subsequent voice tests. Timbre, rather than range, should determine whether he should eventually be classified as tenor or bass. If he is classified as tenor, he will have some difficulty at first with notes around high E and F, until he learns how to produce the highest notes of his range. A boy who has had difficulties of this kind can be lost for good as a tenor unless he receives proper guidance during his high school years. Nature's way of making a tenor is not always a smooth one, and it is a long-drawn-out process.

EFFECT OF THE LONG VACATION

When an adolescent boy stops singing for any length of time, for example, during the summer vacation, there will be a greater change in his voice by the time the vacation is over than there would have been had he kept on singing by reason of being in school. The greatest change will be observed in the voice that is developing into bass. If it was at the alto-tenor stage, or in some cases only at the alto stage, at the beginning of the vacation, very likely by the end of the vacation the changed voice will have developed. The extent of the change varies with the individual voice. But if it is changing to tenor, the change that takes place during the summer vacation is generally very slight, whether the voice is at the alto or the alto-tenor stage.

· 5 ·

Passing from the Unchanged to the Changed Voice

When the changed voice first develops, the boy is still able to sing in his unchanged voice. In singing a descending scale, some boys are able to pass from the unchanged to the changed voice without a break. Others can sing in the unchanged voice down to a certain note, and then there is a break in passing into the changed voice. This difficulty is inherent in voices which are developing into bass, because the mutation is a relatively sudden one, but it need not last for any length of time if the boy has previously used his voice correctly. In most cases the problem of the break can soon be overcome if a definite technique is applied. Boys whose voices are developing into tenor are not so subject to this difficulty; and if the voice has been, and is being, used correctly, there should be no break.

"MANIPULATING" THE VOICE IN THE BREAK AREA

In every boy's voice there is a "break area" when the changed voice begins to develop. This area is where the lower part of the alto-tenor range overlaps the upper part of the changed voice range. It is generally a few notes below and above middle C for voices which are developing into bass; and for voices which are developing into tenor, the upper limit is around E or F (above middle C). If the lowest note of the unchanged voice range is below the highest note of the changed voice range, it is possible to train a boy to sing a descending scale and pass from the unchanged to the changed voice without any break.

Since the boy likes to experiment with his changed voice and will use it in preference to his unchanged voice in any informal singing he does outside the classroom, he will realize there is a certain range within which he can sing with ease in his changed voice. With the help of his teacher, the highest note of this range should be determined, along with the lowest note of the range of his unchanged voice. Knowing this, a boy is ready for the definite vocal technique that will be used in class to meet any difficulty that may occur in the "break area" as he passes from the unchanged to the changed voice. The following is one procedure that can be used.

A scale is chosen in which the first two or three notes of the upper part are in the comfortable range of the unchanged voice and above the break area—any scale between D and F, say. The boy is asked to sing the scale downward, starting in the unchanged voice, decreasing the tone as he approaches the area where the ranges overlap, bringing the unchanged voice down as low as possible, and then "manipulating" it so that he passes into the changed voice. Then he is told to continue the scale, still singing softly. When he feels he is singing with ease in his changed voice, he can increase the volume of tone. If a boy has experienced a break and knows the area where it has occurred, he knows where he has to be careful. If the break occurs on one note at one attempt and on another at the next attempt, it is better to try to do the manipulation at the lower note.

If the comfortable changed voice range is E to B or C' (bass clef) and the boy can sing E or F (above middle C) easily in his unchanged voice, the scale of E or F would do. Provided he can bring his unchanged voice down to A (below middle C)—which he should be able to do because the range of his changed voice has developed so little as yet—he should sing in his unchanged voice down to A, aiming to pass into the changed voice on this note. Because he is singing softly and B (bass clef) is in his changed voice range, he may have passed into the changed voice at B, although aiming to pass into it at A.

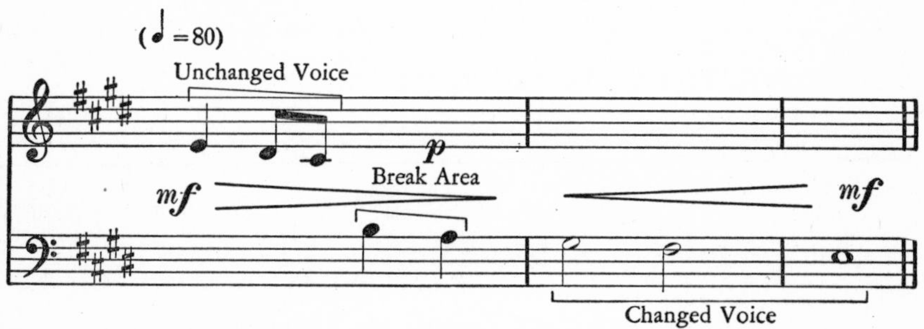

Passing from the Unchanged to the Changed Voice

The best way to describe the manipulation to a boy who cannot manage it at first is to have him listen to and then imitate a boy who can. A few minutes spent during a lesson is all that is necessary. The main thing is to give the boy an opportunity to practice the manipulation, and in carrying out the procedure, he will realize that it is easier if the mind is in control of the voice. Once he has had the experience, "passing" should be made a habit while the upper notes of the changed voice are developing and maturing.

YODELING AS A VOCAL TECHNIQUE

Another plan to overcome the break is to use the "yodel" manner of singing. In *Grove's Dictionary,* "yodel" is described as "the term applied to the abrupt but not inharmonious changes from the chest voice to the falsetto, which are such a well known feature of Tyrolese singers. . . . The practice is not easy to acquire unless the voice has been accustomed to it from early youth. . . . The yodels are not sung to words, but are merely vocalized." At the mutation stage the boy's voice is in a condition that makes yodeling easy for him. Indeed it is more than likely that he has indulged in it. Boys who have developed considerable facility in yodeling can be very helpful in demonstrating this technique in such a phrase as the one below.

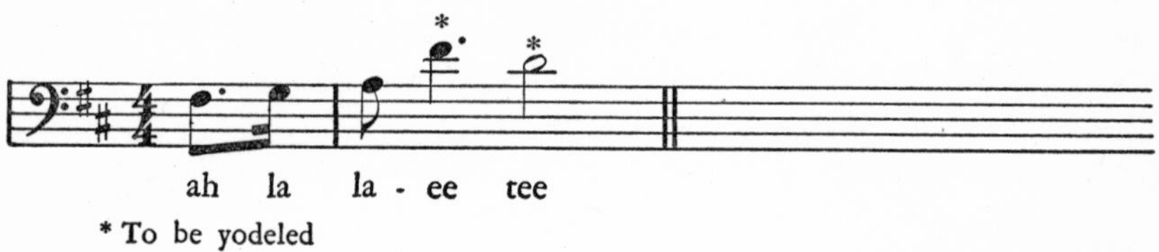

* To be yodeled

Yodeling phrases of songs is a preparation that will enable a boy to sing a bass part that goes outside of the range of his changed voice (see examples). As a matter of vocal technique, the yodeling should be brought as low as possible.

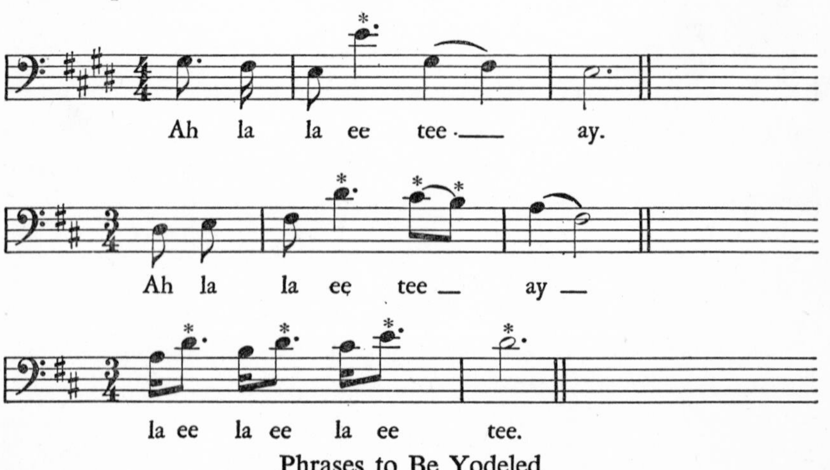

Phrases to Be Yodeled

Knowing the comfortable range of his changed voice, the boy learns to recognize passages in a bass part which he will have to sing falsetto (in the yodeling manner), and after he has had sufficient experience in passing from the falsetto to the changed voice or vice versa, he will do so when he finds it necessary. The use of this vocal technique eliminates the high note problem for the young bass until his upper notes develop and he can sing them easily.

CONTROLLING A GAP

There may be a few notes in the middle of a descending scale that a boy cannot sing at all; that is, there may be a gap. If there is a gap, the boy should not be asked to take part in the vocal exercises just described, but for some time he should sing only in the comfortable range of his changed voice. This means that the part of his unchanged voice which remains is not being used. As the changed voice develops, however, its range increases at both ends, upward much more slowly than downward. Only when the upper range has developed into the area of the gap and the boy can sing with ease in this area, is he ready to sing the vocal exercises designed to overcome the break.

Sometimes, with voices that change suddenly, the gap is as wide as an octave. The boy skips an octave singing a descending scale, thus:

While there is some lack of control for a time in some voices, under ordinary circumstances there is never at any time complete loss of control in any voice. Accordingly, the boy can sing during the period when the mutation is taking place.

DEVELOPING THE UPPER BASS RANGE

When the bass voice has developed so that the boy has a comfortable range of approximately C to C' (middle C) and when the problem of the break has been overcome, it is time to attend to the extension and development of the upper range. The lower part of the unchanged voice which remains should now be called the falsetto voice. This part becomes the upper part of the bass voice as it develops and matures tonally. If a boy were not to use the lower part of his falsetto voice for some time, the upper notes of the bass range would be difficult to produce as they began to develop. On the other hand the boy who has been trained to master the technique for passing from the old voice to the new, and vice versa, does not have difficulty. The basis of the training to develop the upper bass range is downward vocal exercises, but instead of bringing the falsetto voice down as low as possible, the aim should be to pass into the changed voice as high as possible. As the voice matures, the boy is able to pass in a descending scale from the falsetto to the changed voice at a higher note than he could previously. Without training he would force the notes if they were difficult, or he would avoid them altogether.

· 6 ·

Voice Testing

The voice test serves several important purposes. It is used to determine the voice classification for choral work, to discover whether the voice is being used correctly, to reveal any bad habits that may be developing, and to single out pupils who are especially talented. For the boy, the voice testing phase of the music lesson should be a matter of deep personal import, because it enables him to follow the evolution of his adult voice. For the teacher, properly conducted voice testing, considered from a long-range point of view, lays a foundation for the high school choral program.

Every boy should be tested at least twice a year (at the beginning of each semester) while he is in the junior high school. If he can be tested more often, so much the better. Voices that call for frequent testing are those which are changing quickly and those which reveal faults of production.

SAMPLE TESTS

The test itself should be suited to the individual. The same applies to classes, for a test that suits one class may not suit another. It is necessary, therefore, to have a variety of tests on hand.

Example 1 is a test that is used in the sixth grade in many schools. If the pupils have been accustomed to it, it may be well to use it at the start with seventh grade classes. However, there are two objections to it: it is too long, and its range is too wide for most boys in seventh grade classes. Because of its wide range, some boys will be unable to reach the

Example 1

highest notes and will then have to start again and sing the downward scale, some perhaps being unable to reach the bottom notes. The stopping and starting are not conducive to putting a boy at his ease, so he does not do himself justice; nor does he sing enough to allow a satisfactory diagnosis of his voice to be made.

A shorter test, one which suits the majority of changing and changed voices in any grade of the junior high school, is given in Example 2; the b. and c. parts can be used when the boy is able to sing them. If the key of B flat does not suit the individual voice, another key must be found by trial and error.

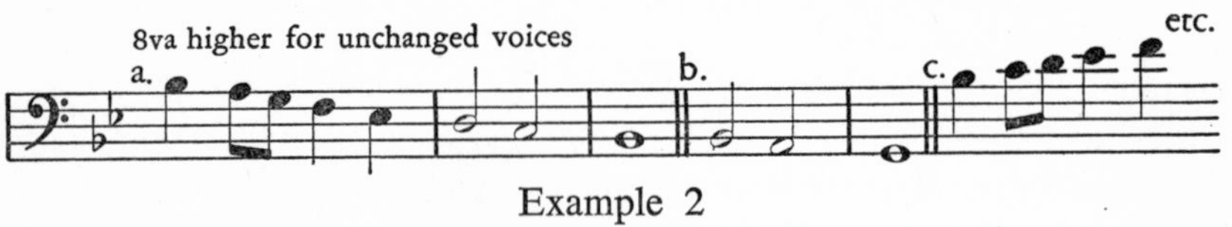

Example 2

Useful as a test or as an addition to the test is a song or part of a song that the boy knows, for some boys make a better showing when they sing a song. The teacher should be ready to make suggestions and to transpose the song or the part of the song to be sung to a key which suits the voice being tested. Songs with a range of less than an octave should be chosen for the voice which is at the alto or the alto-tenor stage, and for the bass voice which has just changed. Otherwise, songs with a range of an octave or a ninth can be used. The song is particularly useful with the talented student, as it affords him a better medium than the scale to show his potentialities. The song should be accompanied. For other types of tests an accompaniment may or may not be used, at the discretion of the teacher; it is better to have the ordinary test sung without accompaniment, but if an accompaniment helps to make the boy more confident and at ease, one should be supplied.

THE IMPORTANCE OF REHEARSING THE TESTS

As voice testing is such an important phase of the music lesson in the junior high school, it is important that a boy's first experiences with it leave a favorable impression and that his interest be aroused. Otherwise, it is not easy to create a good attitude towards testing as a part of a lesson. Hence, before starting individual testing in a seventh grade class, the test to be used should be rehearsed. The rehearsal should be short, but long enough to focus attention on the main points that will help a boy to make a good showing in the individual test. For example, as many of the following points as possible should be touched on: (*1*) It is well to think ahead of what has to be sung; when the mind is in control, better results are obtained than when it is not. (*2*) Attention to good posture and control of the breath are necessary to get good results. (*3*) Good tone is produced only when it is intended. (*4*) Forcing is bad; high notes especially should never be forced.

SOLVING MINOR DIFFICULTIES

Some problems that may be encountered in testing the voice which is at the mutation stage are difficulty in getting the starting note of the test and difficulty in finding the singing voice. Although these difficulties are minor ones, and as a rule temporary, it is well for the teacher to be prepared for them and to know how to help the boy, not so much for his sake as for the sake of the lesson. Often the difficulty is psychological rather than vocal; the boy it not at ease in his new surroundings among new classmates. The difficulty of finding the singing voice will be encountered mainly in a seventh grade class among the older boys whose voices have just changed. Generally they will be boys of superior physique but inferior intellect. Some may be able to sing in both the unchanged and the changed voice, but not at will. The reason may be physical (because the larynx growth is too sudden for the mechanism), or mental, if the boy does not have the capacity of putting his mind in control of his voice. In either case, the boy should be tested privately. The difficulty will then disappear when dealt with in class, provided that the lessons are effective.

The difficulty of getting the starting note of a test may be due to the ear rather than to the voice. If so, encourage the boy to take full advantage of any ear training that may be done in class. More often, however, the difficulty is linked to some adolescent trait, such as shyness and lack of confidence, or nervousness. The boy does not have complete control of his faculties. He cannot think the sound of the starting note; or he may have lost the feeling of the tonality of the test. Such a boy needs some attention, unobtrusive and incidental, in the class lessons, so that at the next test he will feel he is ready to make a better showing.

Because these difficulties are common, they can be dealt with to some extent during the rehearsal of the test by giving hints on how to overcome them. Thus a boy who experiences difficulty in the class singing of the test and has been given some inkling of what to do about it is better prepared when he comes to sing by himself. The first appearance of any difficulty in the individual testing should be used as an opportunity for a short lesson, to show the boy that his difficulties are understood. A sympathetic attitude on the part of the teacher will build up a faith that influences the attitude of a class and makes the boys in it want to cooperate.

Since voice testing consumes time, a routine should be established to prevent unnecessary loss of time. For example, when a boy has difficulty with the starting note, the class should sing the note without being asked. When he gets it, a signal should be given to the class to stop singing and the boy should go on alone. If nervousness is the trouble, have the class sing with the boy until he gets started, and then, again on a signal, the class should stop.

TIME BUDGET FOR VOICE TESTING

The amount of time to be devoted to testing calls for careful consideration. From the point of view of the general music lesson, several matters have to be noted. Is there a definite program laid down for the general music lesson? If so, what is the relative importance attached to singing as compared with other phases? If there is no definite program, as is very often the case, what is the teacher's attitude towards adolescent boys in choral work? What is the grade of the class? If it is a seventh grade, what musical background do the pupils bring with them from the grade school; if it is an eighth or ninth grade, do many new students enter the school in these grades?

Let us consider the time question first of all as it relates to a class of boys only, although such classes are rare in the junior high school. One advantage that a boys' class has over a mixed class is that a continuity of interest in the work can be maintained. This makes for a better classroom atmosphere, in which testing can be made so engrossing a topic that there need never be a time when interest lags. This interest is necessary, for testing is part of the regular business of a lesson, and a considerable amount must always be done. Retesting, which is often unexpectedly required, will not spoil the continuity of a lesson if the students are interested in it.

In a mixed class the time budget allowed for testing boys' voices depends a good deal on the interest and attitude shown by the girls. Once they begin to lose interest, it is time to stop testing and take up one of the other phases of the lesson—sight-reading, ear training, music appreciation.

Testing should be carried out as expeditiously as possible, but also as thoroughly as possible. "The more hurry, the less speed" can be aptly applied to testing, for on its thoroughness and effectiveness hinges the success of nursing the boy's voice during the change. Singing should be considered basic in all the phases of the lesson and voice testing an essential to make the singing enjoyable. Retesting is also a part of any lesson, performed when necessary to help a boy over a difficulty. Obviously, more time will be required for testing in a seventh grade than in a higher grade, especially at the beginning of the session; but allowance must also be made for it in the eighth and ninth grades, particularly if new pupils enter these grades. Another factor in determining a time budget for testing is the number of periods a week allotted to music.

Voice testing may take on a considerable importance in the general music program if it is thought of in connection with the choral organizations. This does not mean, however, that more time should be devoted to it at the expense of the other phases of the lesson. The teacher's attitude towards the different phases will have a good deal to do with the time budget for testing. The attitude may lean to working for choral results, or it may lean to developing general musicianship through the music appreciation lesson. Whatever it is, the testing should be regarded from a long-range point of view, in relation to the year's program as well as to the boy's vocal future.

THE VOICE CARD

It is advisable to keep a voice card for every boy, to record his voice history from the time he enters the junior high school. A card such as

VOICE CARD

Name.............................. Date of birth.............

School last attended...

....

....

Date	Height	Weight	Full Range	Comfortable Range	Classification	Grading	Remarks

the one illustrated provides for all the information that it is desirable to record.

Without some kind of card system, a teacher cannot hope to estimate the potentialities of a class for the purposes of choral work and appraise the material in the class. While he will not be able to remember a great deal about many of the voices tested, the voice card enables him to individualize some. Accordingly, he knows both what can and what should not be demanded from certain students. Keeping voice histories may be considered a part of the choral program.

For the teacher with little experience, the voice card is indispensable. It disciplines him to make a diagnosis of a voice and trains him to be more observant than he might otherwise be. The card also has a value for the boy; it keeps him informed and should arouse his interest in the progress of his voice. The boy may not, and most likely will not, remember many of the details recorded at the different tests, but a comparison of one diagnosis with another cannot but whet his curiosity. This will induce him to become observant, and he will want to report of his own accord any signs of development or any difficulty he encounters. Difficulties can then be treated as they arise instead of after they have been discovered in the testing.

Some comments about the headings on the voice card follow.

Recording the name of the school last attended by a pupil is of value only if something is known about the musical instruction given in that school. For instance, if the teacher knows how well reading has been taught, or the standard of the class singing, a propitious start can be made with seventh grade classes without any break in the continuity of the instruction. The early lessons, therefore, can be devoted to the new problems that boys have in the seventh grade.

After the name of the school last attended there may be entered such information as the following: instrument studied and length of time of study; choir experience in school or church; information about musical conditions in the home. This information can be obtained by means of a questionnaire; it helps to individualize a pupil.

It is advisable to record both the full and the comfortable ranges at each test, and definite criteria should be set up for determining them. For the full range, the criteria should be a certain tonal development, with ease of production at the upper and lower limits. As it is important for the boy to know his comfortable range throughout the adolescent period, he should understand the criteria set up, so that when he finds he can sing outside his comfortable range he will report it. In this way the boy keeps a closer check on his voice than the teacher can.

To grade, or make an appraisal of the caliber and tonal development of a voice, the following scheme is suggested, with a system for noting it on the voice card:

Caliber of Voice	*Tonal Development*
A—shows signs of promise	*a*—very good
B—above the average	*b*—good
C—the average voice	*c*—fair
D—below the average	*d*—very little

Cb would mean, therefore, a voice of average caliber with good tonal development. If grading is to be used in connection with glee clubs, the more promising voices can be further identified by adding a plus or minus to either or both letters of the grades.

Grading not only sharpens the teacher's powers of observation but also enables him to check the results of training between tests. For the boy, grading should be an incentive to aim for a better mark. When a low grade is given, the reason for it should be entered in the "Remarks" column. Team spirit can be aroused by seating a class by grades, and different grades of a part can compete rehearsing a passage. This will give momentum to the rehearsal.

The purpose of the "Remarks" is to record observations that will be of future value. Though the remarks will be mainly about faults, bad habits, and voice difficulties, anything that can be commended should also be recorded, for a word of praise helps to establish a bond of fellowship with the boy. The remarks help to individualize a voice. The problem is to devise a system of codes that will give the maximum amount of information with the minimum amount of writing. The meaning of the codes should be explained to the class as the necessity for using them arises. When it is necessary to record a remark that would embarrass the pupil being tested, it should be made clear that certain codes are for the teacher's use only.

To facilitate the work of recording, a secretary may be trained for every class. It is well to select a pupil who can write quickly, neatly, and legibly, one who requires little attention after the initial training.

The following are suggested codes for the "Remarks" column:

ATMT gd: a good attempt.

A good attempt should always be commended, whatever the caliber and development of the voice, for it shows that the pupil's attitude is right. Such a boy has a wholesome influence in a class and will make good material for the glee club, even though his talent may be average. If a boy makes a poor attempt, a reason for it should be sought and the reason recorded in a private code. The boy should receive some individual, but incidental, attention in class to help him to make a better attempt at the next test. A private test may be considered advisable if a reason cannot be discerned at the test given in class.

D: diffident (private code).

A poor showing may be the result of diffidence arising from various factors. For example, it may be caused by some adolescent trait, or it may be due to a wrong attitude towards testing; if the latter, the teacher must try to counteract this before the next test, for one boy with the wrong attitude can spoil the atmosphere of a lesson.

DCN gd: diction good.

As good diction is so uncommon with adolescent boys, it should always be commended, and the boy can be used as a model for others to follow.

F: forcing.

Record the part of the range in which the voice is being forced; also the consequences of the forcing, such as throatiness.

FAL: falsetto range.

In recording the falsetto range, note whether the boy passes from the changed to the falsetto or vice versa, with or without a break. If there is a break, record where it occurs and whether in an ascending or a descending scale passage. For example, *FAL:* B, to E (treble clef) by itself means that this is the falsetto range and there is no break singing an ascending or a descending scale. If there is a break at middle C, say, singing an ascending scale, record thus: *FAL:* B, to E; break at C, ascending. And if there is also a break at B, singing a descending scale, record thus: *FAL:* B, to E; break at C, ascending; B, descending.

N: nervous (private code).

A boy who is nervous should never be asked to sing a test before a class against his will. He should be tested in private.

PV: promising voice.

The promising changed voice should be particularly noted so that no bad habits are allowed to develop. A boy with a good voice likes to sing; he needs guidance as to the type of songs he should and should not sing. Accordingly, he should be encouraged to bring his songs for a hearing either in class or privately.

RET: report for a retest at a certain date because of some "remark" that has been recorded.

T: tone, with some additional remark, such as nasal, throaty, resonant, or nonresonant.

Other observations worth recording are the status of the talking voice (*TV*) compared with that of the singing voice (*SV*), especially at the alto-tenor stage; and peculiarities of diction due to nationality or the influence of a dialect the boy has been accustomed to hear and use. Such peculiarities are not in themselves bad, but they are bad if they lead to wrong production in singing because of the distortion of vowels.

It is helpful to record as much information as possible on the voice card at each test; however, the time element will usually make it impracticable to use all the columns. Any omissions may be filled in at later tests. The full and comfortable ranges, at least, should be entered at every test. Noting the difference in the full range between tests is a guide in observing the rate at which the voice is changing (lowering in pitch). It should be a policy to make some entry in the "Remarks" column at every test, especially if it will be of value for the future.

· 7 ·

Tonal Possibilities in the Junior High School Chorus

REHEARSAL TECHNIQUES

In the junior high school, the nature of the material found among the boys is just about as heterogeneous as it could be, in terms of the boys' voices and their musicianship. On the other hand, the working conditions of the class lesson are about as ideal as they can be from the standpoint of rehearsal procedure.

In a church choir or a choral society, rehearsal procedure generally consists in learning the music and "putting in" the expression. This "putting in" is a rough and ready way of getting interpretation; the expression is imposed. The conductor stops the rehearsal to give such instructions as "swell this note or passage," "accent such and such notes." No reason is given usually, nor is one sought. This way of getting interpretation is superficial, not musical, and it contributes little to the understanding of the music and the enjoyment of rehearsing. Indeed the interruptions tend to become irksome, especially to those singers who, having learned the music, are ready to make it deliver its message. The finer points of choral singing are not treated, usually for lack of time. This type of rehearsing does not lay the foundations for fine choralism.

In the junior high school, there is no significant pressure to prepare a certain amount of music within a certain time. Consequently, time can be allowed for dealing intelligently with many of the finer points that make for superior choral work. These points can be dealt with in rehearsal in short lessons, introduced when occasion demands or according to plan, as an integral part of the rehearsal procedure. For example, a rehearsal often has to be stopped to correct a mistake or to learn a passage. The interruption can be used to observe the passage in some special way, so that the singers will be better prepared to give it a musical rather than a superficial rendering. By commenting on a passage in its "mental effect" aspect,[1] say, a deeper concentration on such matters as color, blend, and atmosphere can be obtained. Or, if an interruption is required because of a fault in tone production, some individual voice testing may be necessary to discover the individual or individuals responsible for the fault. Depending on what happens in the testing, the interruption can be further used as the excuse for short lessons on points in tone production. A topic that can be made the basis of many such lessons is the effect and function of dissonace, examples of different kinds being taken from the music as it is being learned.

The potential number, as well as the variety, of short lessons that can arise out of the usual interruptions that occur in a rehearsal is unlimited. It is through the lessons that choral technique can be developed; and while it is better to introduce them according to plan, there should be no hesitation in introducing them according to inspiration. The incidental short lesson freshens the atmosphere of a rehearsal. "Spiritual considerations can almost be left to themselves if technical foundations are well and truly laid. What is lacking in singers is not sensibility and imagination, but simply efficient workmanship." [2]

THE CONDUCTOR'S CONCEPT

The standard of choral results possible with a group of any kind—children, adolescents, or adults—is never higher than the conductor's concept of what is possible with the group. What can be accomplished with a junior high school group depends first of all on the concept of the tonal possibilities of adolescent voices, especially the boys' voices. The question has several ramifications. The general caliber of the vocal material is important, but it must be remembered that a junior high school group differs from any other in that the status of the boys' voices is constantly changing in range and tone quality. Thus the tonal possibilities must not be thought of in terms of the more mature but still adolescent voices of high school boys, especially with reference to the alto-tenor section. A junior high school alto-tenor section cannot be trained to sound like a high school tenor section, even if it has in it a considerable number of alto-tenors.

The matter of voice preservation also has a bearing on the question. In the junior high school the emphasis should be on voice preservation rather than on voice training. This is so in the high school, too, though

[1] The doctrine of "mental effects" was originated by John Curwen, the founder of the Tonic Solfa Method. It is explained in his *Musical Theory* (London, Curwen; New York, G. Schirmer).

[2] Charles Kennedy Scott, *Madrigal Singing* (London, Oxford University Press, 1931). Mr. Scott discusses "The Expression of Dissonance" in a way that offers suggestions for a series of short lessons.

not to the same extent, for most of the voices have passed through the critical stage of the mutation, and a certain amount of voice training is beneficial for those boys whose voices have changed and developed to a comfortable range of an octave. There will of course be voice training in the junior high school, but it will be incidental, as necessity demands in order to get some immediate result. Excerpts from the music being learned will be used, not formal voice exercises. The latter have no place in the junior high school, for psychological, if not vocal, reasons. Whatever incidental voice training is done should be thought of in terms of voice preservation.

It is particularly necessary to keep the matter of preservation in mind once a changed voice begins to show evidence of developing into one above average. A great deal of harm can be done if a boy has a voice teacher who has not had experience with adolescent voices and deals with him as though he were an adult. At contests it is not uncommon to come across a promising changed, but still adolescent, voice which shows signs of being spoiled because of the way the boy has been trained to sing. Voice preservation is more important than vocal results for some time to come; the more it is taken into consideration the more favorable are the chances of getting results later. In the junior high school, it is the promising young bass who has to be watched, for the tenor does not develop till he gets into high school. It is to be remembered that although a voice has potentialities at every stage of the adolescent period, it also has its limitations.

Factors other than voice should also be taken into account in forming a concept of the tonal possibilities of a group. Chief among them are the general and musical intelligence of the student and his ability to read music, as well as the amount of time per lesson devoted to singing. The better the musicianship of the individual student, the better member of the group he is. A well-integrated music program will raise the standard as the students pass from grade to grade; hence the importance of the various phases of the general music lesson.

WORKING FOR GOOD TONE

Good tone is a primary requisite in choral singing. Without it, there cannot be good interpretation, no matter how fine the singing is in other respects. A conductor must constantly be seeking good tone. To get it he must have the full cooperation of his singers. Consequently, they must have a proper understanding about tone and tone production. With adolescent boys this is a matter of the utmost importance, for it is during the period of the change of voice that the boy can be started in the right or wrong direction for the future. The faculty of imitation being strong, almost anyone who has an ear for tone can learn to sing with good tone by listening to good models and copying them. The problem with adolescent boys is to find good models for the different stages of the changing voice. One solution is for the teacher to make recordings of the best examples encountered during the course of his work.[3] Otherwise, the best that can be found in the groups he is working with must do. The tone of a boys' section in a junior high school is never any better than that of its best models.

It should be noted that an ear for tone is not the same as an ear for tune; the latter has to do with the relation of tones of different pitch (that is, with sight-reading). The ear for tone is analogous to the artist's eye for color. It is developed by listening to the tone of singers, instrumentalists, and instrumental groups (large and small), and appraising it as good or bad. There is no standardized type of tone for the singer, for each individual is differently constituted as to the factors that make up his voice. Voices differ, for instance, in the size of their resonating cavities; good tone in one voice is therefore not the same as good tone in another. Good tone, however, can be recognized in any voice by certain definite characteristics. "To be good, it must be forward; hollow, hooty, throaty, or shouty tone is simply tone that has not been projected forward. To be forward, tone must be free from muscular restrictions (the throat, the tongue, and the jaw are the chief offenders here). Then it must be resonant. . . . White tone, dull tone, shallow tone, is all tone in which resonators are not functioning adequately."[4] Learning to recognize the characteristics of good tone is an essential part of the singer's training. The right kind of listening, with the right kind of guidance in making an appraisal, develops the faculty of discrimination; and as the discriminative powers become more keen, the student is able to detect fine shades and textures of tone.

Singing is a natural manifestation, and it should be considered as such. In training the adolescent voice there is no place for the jargon of the studio—for instance, saying that the tone should be placed in the mask. Rather, the sounds made in games to express feelings of joy, anger, excitement, and so on, should be made the basis of a natural technique. This technique is attained by building upon the reflex and other actions that nature provides originally for vital purposes, not artistic purposes; yawning (in relation to getting the right conditions for resonance), smelling a flower (in dealing with breathing).

[3] It is suggested that a boy whose voice is to be recorded give his name, his age, height, and weight, as well as his classification, so that the status of his speaking voice may be noted with reference to the status of his singing voice.

[4] Hugh Roberton, *Mixed Voice Choirs; Female Voice Choirs; Male Voice Choirs* (London, Paterson, 1923; New York, Carl Fischer).

A boy should be encouraged to experiment with his voice, for example to sing with good or with bad tone, at will. Only when he can do so, does he have control of his voice; control is the aim of training. Developing good tone is easier for the adolescent boy than for the adult, for the adult does not care to experiment with his voice; it is unnatural for him to try to. Unfortunately, the boy's interest in certain types of singing—crooning and similar vogues—makes the task of developing good tone somewhat of a problem; it is psychological at first, but in the end aural. Crooning, for instance, is neither a good model nor a good style to imitate. Hence it is important to increase the boy's powers of appraisal and discrimination. The ear gives the right or wrong instructions to the vocal mechanism: to the muscles used in breathing and to the voice in phonation and diction. In other words, the ear is the organ in control of the voice.

One of the commonest faults in singing is throatiness. It results from a contraction of the swallowing muscles. The normal use of these muscles consists in a strong contraction lasting a short time, followed by rest. If they are contracted for any length of time while singing, they tire, and the throat aches. Thus the whole act of singing is encumbered. Throatiness usually occurs in the singer's attempt to sing high notes outside of the comfortable range, an aching sensation being felt if it is done too often.

THE ALTO-TENOR SECTION

In the junior high school, the alto-tenor section is the most difficult one to work with because the quickly changing voices are invariably more numerous than the slowly changing ones; the former do not remain in the alto-tenor section for any length of time. They also have difficulty in managing their voices, a difficulty which is inherent in the quickly changing voice. Demands made at rehearsals must therefore be reasonable. Too often vocal difficulties as well as vocal limitations are ignored.

Why are poor results heard so often from a junior high school alto-tenor section? One reason might be that the section does not receive sufficient attention; another, that it remains intact for so short a time it is not thought worth while to devote much attention to it. If this is the attitude, it should be remembered that it is at the alto-tenor stage that a boy can be won or lost insofar as his future interest in choral singing is concerned. If he gets off to a bad start, he may lose any interest he has had. Consequently, he is lost for the high school choral organizations. A more common reason for poor singing from the alto-tenors is the lack of a concept of the tonal possibilities of the section. In any junior high school alto-tenor section the individual voices would be rated ordinary, many of them so ordinary that one would think the choral possibilities were very limited; however, it is surprising what can be done with them as a group. If the rehearsal procedure is of a kind to make the boys feel that progress is being made and they sense that results are in the making, the potentialities of the section are being revealed to them.

Because he experiences a new power in his voice as an alto-tenor, it is natural for a boy to glory in this power—and he does. He sings more strenuously than he should; the result is raucous tone, due to forcing. To prevent the development of bad tone in the alto-tenor section, any sign of raucous tone in the alto section should be checked immediately. This means that special attention must be given to the individuals responsible. Unfortunately school conditions (large classes and lack of time) are not favorable for a great deal of individual attention; the boy himself must be trained to realize his responsibility, not so much for the sake of choral results as for the sake of his future voice.

How can the boy be made to realize his responsibility? One way is by individual voice testing, for it enables him to understand what is happening to his voice. Moreover, he observes other boys being tested; he notes their difficulties and problems, and how they are solved. The testing interests him. In other words, the boy himself can develop a concept of his part in the training; he must understand his potentialities as well as his limitations.

The tone to have in mind as the ideal is one that is contralto-like in character. It has no trace of adult tenor timbre, and it lacks virility; but it has its own peculiar timbre—that associated with the voice at the youth stage. In the upper range it can be quite effective, though in the lower it is ineffective; but as the quickly changing voice develops tonally during the course of a session, it becomes effective to a degree. Volume should not be sought; the intensity can be stepped up when it is considered safe to do so, but forcing must not be allowed. Should there be an adolescent (changed voice) tenor in the section (as occasionally there may be), his presence will make itself felt when the part is in the lower range.

If an alto-tenor section is made up of selected voices, a fairly accurate estimate of its tonal possibilities can be made, depending on whether it is to remain more or less intact for a semester or a year; if for a year, there would need to be a greater proportion of slowly changing voices, whereas if for a semester, an equal number of slowly changing and quickly changing voices could be selected. Quickly changing voices should not be rejected on the ground that they do not remain alto-tenor for any length of time. Although voices of good caliber should be sought, voice quality should not be the main consideration. Reading ability and musical intelligence should be factors in the selection. For a section made up of selected voices it is possible to approximate the ideal one has in mind, even though the concept will change during the course of the semester because of the quickly changing voices.

THE BASS SECTION

The tonal ideal to conceive of in a bass section is tone that is characteristically bass, but immature bass, since it is evident that the voices are unsettled and will remain unsettled during the junior high school years. As the boys grow older, their tone becomes more mature. The tonal possibilities of the section, therefore, change during the course of the session towards the ideal which has been conceived. A good bass section is always possible, especially when the voices are selected.

THE MIXED VOICE CHORUS

The tone of a junior high school mixed voice chorus, even one of selected voices, sounds quite unlike that of any other type of mixed voice chorus. It can be compared to a high school chorus in some ways: the difference in the soprano and bass sections, especially the latter, is one of maturity tonally; and there is little difference between the alto sections. A junior high school alto-tenor section, however, cannot be compared with a high school tenor section, even if there are alto-tenors in the latter, because of the absence of changed voice tone. It is this absence of changed voice tone in the alto-tenor section that gives the junior high school mixed voice chorus its peculiar character.

To estimate the tonal possibilities of a grade classified for mixed voice work, several things have to be taken into consideration. Singing is only one phase of the music lesson, and in two or three periods a week there is not a great deal of time for choral work. This work is of a foundational nature; choral results are in the making. The aim is to build up an interest and liking for choral work. The training should be regarded as the climax of the general music lesson, the result of the cumulative effect of all its phases. One of the problems is to get balance of parts. Balance can be obtained with selected voices, but not with a class—not even with a ninth grade class where conditions are more favorable than in the lower grades.

Consider an eighth or ninth grade class in which there are equal numbers of boys and girls, all the boys being in the alto-tenor and bass sections. A fairly good balance is possible between the soprano and alto sections, and between the soprano and bass sections. The alto-tenor section is the weakest tonally, and it is likely to be the smallest in number. Furthermore, it will get smaller during the session as some boys are transferred to bass. Balance is therefore impossible. But no matter how unbalanced a class may be, it should undergo the discipline necessary to find out what balance in choral work means and how it is obtained. The junior high school is the place where this training should be started, and here is one plan that will give the students some actual experience.

For a short composition (two or three pages) a scale of dynamics is worked out in terms of the weakest part, the alto-tenor, say. A *mezzo forte* for the alto-tenors would be a *mezzo* for the basses; also for the sopranos if they numbered approximately the same as the bass section. From this would be determined the dynamics for the altos. This scale of dynamics could be stepped up or down as necessary; for example, *forte* for the alto-tenors, *mezzo forte* for the sopranos and basses, the alto possibly having to sing *mezzo* or *mezzo forte*. Later in the session the scale would have to be adjusted to suit the changes that occurred in the classifications of the boys and in the tonal development of the various sections.

While it is the conductor's business to get balance, the singers must understand their responsibility in the matter. Each one must get into the habit of listening to the ensemble and regulate his tone himself in addition to regulating it as asked by the conductor. Balance does not depend altogether on the number of singers to the part. Generally speaking, the soprano part overwhelms the other parts; and the bass does not make itself felt as it should. The bass part, Hugh Roberton says, "should be a floating bass. . . . Even in the final cadences there should be a feeling of the bass holding up or bearing the other parts, like a proud galleon bearing a rich cargo." The inner parts are as a rule the least effective; they should receive more attention than is generally given to them, especially at places where certain notes should be brought out to intensify the color of the harmony: for example, the third of a major or minor chord, the fourth and seventh of the scale in a dominant seventh chord, chromatic notes, nonharmony notes in dissonant chords. A weaker part can always be made to register if the mental effects of certain notes are exaggerated.

· 8 ·

Preserving the Pre-Tenor Voice

Should tenors be as scarce as they are? In considering this question, two facts should be kept in mind. First, tenors in adult choral organizations are always scarce and, second, the tenor voice is slow in developing.

During the junior high school years, a boy's voice can, at a certain stage, be labeled "changing slowly" or "changing quickly," and the latter type is always more numerous than the former. Tenors come from the slowly changing type. Once a voice can be labeled "slowly changing," it should be regarded as a potential tenor, and it should be dealt with as if it were going to be tenor up to the time when it shows it will not be one. The question to be considered might therefore be: Are any potential tenors lost during the junior high school years because of current procedure?

Vocal procedure in the junior high school is based on the premises that the principles of voice training which have proved best with the boy's voice in the grade school—namely, downward training—are the best to use with the adolescent boy's voice; and that because of the continuity in the method of training, the boy is able to sing during the adolescent period. Obviously, the better the training during the preadolescent period, the better the chance of success in preserving the boy's voice during the change. Many of the problems that arise during the change can be referred back to the preadolescent period.

Because the junior high school has mixed classes, the S.A.T.B. (T. being Alto-Tenor) classification is the most practical one for choral work. The problem that this classification creates is that it is not possible to maintain an alto-tenor section for any length of time because of the quickly changing voices. The alto-tenor whose voice is changing slowly, however, remains in the classification for a considerable length of time. Because he is able to sing in the alto range for some time after he is classified as alto-tenor, he could be used as an alto in a boys' choir singing S.S.A. music. But boys' choirs are not common in the junior high school.

One thing in favor of the boys' choir in which the alto section is made up of slowly changing voices is that permanency of classification is assured for a year. Hence, there is time to work for results, and one justification for such a choir is that very beautiful results can be obtained from it. Another advantage is that the matter of classifying an alto as alto-tenor does not arise.

Although the policy of the modern theory about the boy's changing voice is to encourage it to lower, the policy should not be misinterpreted in the case of voices which are changing slowly.[1] Many potential tenors are lost for good by being classified too soon as alto-tenors. There is no harm in having a boy whose voice has reached the alto stage sing the alto-tenor part, provided he uses it correctly, for the ranges of the two parts are practically the same. The trouble is, more often than not, that the voice is not used correctly because the boy is singing in a mixed voice group where he is exposed to influences that are not conducive to the right use of the voice. He is apt to force, and this leads to trouble later on. Forcing the slowly changing voice to lower during the pre-tenor period is just as wrong and as bad for the future voice as trying to retain the upper notes of the range at any stage during the adolescent period.

Classified as alto-tenor too soon, a boy loses control over the upper notes of his range. The result is that if the voice is going to be tenor, these notes will be difficult to sing when he becomes tenor; and if he forces them, he will have trouble around high E and F. It is at this stage—generally the early high school years—that a potential tenor may be lost if he is not properly guided. The boy becomes discouraged at his inability to manage his upper range, so he wants to sing bass. If he is transferred to bass, and if nothing further is done, he may never sing tenor again.

No harm is done by transferring a young tenor to bass if he has been having difficulty with his upper range. As a matter of fact, it is better to transfer him, but the boy has to understand that he is not a bass and that he must sing only in a range which is comfortable. He will be of little use as a bass, and he will soon realize this, for the *tessitura* of the part will be less and less comfortable the longer he sings bass. This is nature's way of warning him that he is in the wrong classification. He should be transferred back to the tenor section, where he will be more comfortable. Thus he has been saved as a tenor. Since he may have difficulty around high F, he must be warned and made to realize that the high notes of the tenor voice are slow in developing, that they will be slower than usual in his case because he has not been using them while singing bass, and that it will take some time to gain control over them.

The highest notes of the alto part in the music used by a boys' choir are not likely to be out of range for the alto-tenor whose voice is changing slowly, and while he sings alto, his voice is developing towards the tenor

[1] The cambiata plan, adapted from the alto-tenor plan by Professor Irvin Cooper, is suitable for the potential tenor. For a discussion of the cambiata see Chapter 10.

status; by the time he reaches the high school, he is ready to be classified as tenor. Consequently, the alto section of a junior high school boys' choir can be a nursery for potential tenors.

In carrying out the alto-tenor plan which prevails in American schools, what can be done to save as much of this potential tenor material as possible? The plan has been in operation for a good many years. It is the most important and far-reaching contribution that the junior high school has made to the choral phase of musical education. It has not only made the choral program that exists today possible, but it has also prepared the way for the current high school program. The vocal phase of the junior high school program, however, has become stereotyped. The only variation that has been introduced into it is the boys' glee club, which is not intended especially for the vocally talented boy, though it has afforded him an opportunity to develop and improve his talent. The extent to which the music program in the junior high school can be valuable to the talented boy is of course limited. The quickly changing voices are in the majority, and though many of them develop into reasonably good basses in the junior high school, they are too unsettled to justify offering any other type of training than that given in the general music lesson and the boys' glee club. On the other hand, the boy whose voice is changing slowly always has a considerable voice range at any stage during the adolescent period, and during the transition period he does not encounter the difficulties of the boy with the quickly changing voice. It might be possible, therefore, to offer him some special training of the type that would be given in the voice class.

A talented boy soprano will continue to have a superior voice as it changes, provided that he continues to use it properly. If he is considered a potential tenor because of his slowly changing voice, the voice class would afford the most favorable conditions to deal with the voice at the most important period of its development to tenor. Whether or not it will be superior in adult life cannot be predicted. Even if it is not, he will be a valuable choir member because of his talent, his previous training, and his experience.

Now that the existing junior high school music program is subject to reevaluation because it has settled into a fixed pattern, there is an opportunity for reshaping it. The potential tenor voice needs more nursing during the pre-tenor stage than it gets in today's program. It should be dealt with in a special group in the voice class. Such classes might prove that tenors are not so scarce after all, and the junior high school would have made another contribution to music education, one that would be of great value to the adult choral society.

· 9 ·

A Selection of Voice Histories

The voice histories given in this chapter are intended to serve as models. They have been selected from records on boys in the Glee Club of the Harding Junior High School, Lakewood, Ohio, who volunteered to stay after rehearsals to be tested several times during the course of a semester or longer. The histories were kept according to the voice card discussed in a previous chapter. The testing was done by Gertrude M. Scott, Head of the Music Department of the school; to her I am indebted for undertaking the project so that it could be used in this study.

Selected for the project were boys who, about a month before the summer vacation, were entering the adolescent period or had just entered it. Their histories were kept up to the end of the first semester following the summer vacation, and to the end of the second semester or longer if the voice was a slowly changing one. Particular note was taken of the early development of the changed voice in the matter of passing from the unchanged to the changed voice, or vice versa. The boys were given an opportunity in the glee club rehearsals to experiment with the training technique described in Chapter 5. Note was also taken of any psychological problems a boy had, if they had a bearing on the development of his voice.

Towards the end of the first semester, Mrs. Scott reported: "Boys whose voices were above average when unchanged had least trouble in covering up the break and passing into the upper range of the changed voice. In most cases the change was almost imperceptible, and the quality of tone in both the unchanged and the changed voice was good. Those who were not of above average caliber musically found it difficult to make the voice adjustment, and there was sometimes a gap of several tones—from a third to an octave—between the old and the new voice. Most of the breaks occurred in the vicinity of middle C. It seemed that the unchanged quality was easier to maintain when singing a descending scale than when singing an ascending one, the range being four or five tones greater for a descending scale."

In the voice histories which follow, capital letters indicate that notes are in the treble clef, small letters that they are in the bass clef. In the illustration below, notes from C (first leger line below the treble staff) to B (third line) are unmarked, a superior symbol being added for notes above B and an inferior figure for notes below C. Similarly in the bass clef, notes from c (second space) to b (first space above the staff) are unmarked, a superior symbol being added for notes above b and an inferior for notes below c.

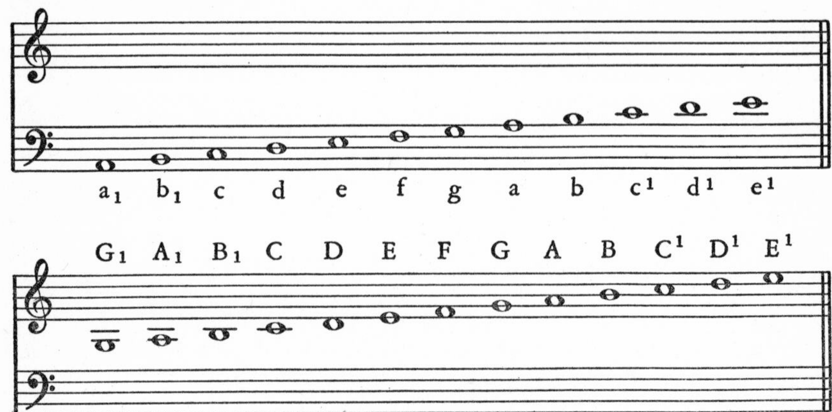

Key to Voice Ranges

CASE A

Although Case A had the range of a Soprano I at the first test, he was classified as Soprano II, because (*1*) the notes in his lower range indicated that the voice had started to lower, and (*2*) the boy said he had put on ten pounds in weight during the few weeks previous to the test—both being evidence of his physiological development.

During the summer and up to mid-October he gained 6.5 pounds in weight, and his height increased 5¼″—a normal growth. From mid-October to the end of the semester, his weight increased 4.5 pounds and his height ¾″, that is, the growth in height had slowed down, while the growth in weight continued at a normal rate.

His range from the start of the summer vacation to the end of the first semester was practically stationary, except for a slight development in the lower range. The voice could therefore be labeled a slowly changing one, and hence a potential tenor. He was classified alto-tenor at the end of the semester because of his age and his grade, though most likely he would have been comfortable singing alto for another semester at least.

CASE B

From June to the end of September, Case B did not gain any weight and his height increased only ½″. Then he gained nine pounds in weight and

Case A: An Eighth Grader Who is a Potential Tenor

Class 8A—Age at First Test: 14 years, 8 months

Studied trumpet for four years; plays in band and sings in school choir. Is a leader in his classification in glee club. Has a fine feeling for music.

Family: Austrian—distant Russian. Mother plays piano quite well. Sister plays piano.

Date of Test	Weight	Height	Physical Appearance	Speaking Voice	Full Range	Comfortable Range	Classification	Remarks
End of June	103	4′ 11¾″	A small boy just beginning to develop.	Inclined to alto in quality; husky.	g to A|	g to F|	Soprano II	Said he had gained ten pounds in the last few weeks.
Mid-October	109.5	5′ 5″	Facial expression more mature; slender.	That of an alto.	f to G|	g to D|	Alto	Smooth quality in singing voice.
Mid-November	115	5′ 5½″	Looks much smaller because of the weight he has put on. Down on upper lip.	That of an alto.	e to G|	f♯ to D|	Alto	Still has smooth quality in singing voice.
End of first semester	114	5′ 5¾″	Slight, youthful expression. Down on face.	That of an alto.	e to G|	f♯ to D|	Alto-Tenor	Not much change.

Case B: The Average Boy Baritone in Grade 8

Class 8B—Age at First Test: 13 years, 6 months

Sang in the grade school choir. Has never studied an instrument.
Family: Mother plays piano fairly well, but for amusement only.

Date of Test	Weight	Height	Physical Appearance	Speaking Voice	Full Range	Comfortable Range	Classification	Remarks
June	113	5′ 8″	Features of a youth.	More alto-tenor than changed. Voice unsettled.	d to D	f to $c^{\prime}$	Baritone	Changed voice developing rapidly. Pitch wavers.
July	113	5′ 8″	Awkward and self-conscious.	Tending away from youth voice to baritone.	$g_{\prime}$ to D	c to a	Baritone	Adolescent baritone. Great change in timbre.
End of September	113	5′ 8½″	Looks older generally.	Voice more settled.	$g_{\prime}$ to b	$g_{\prime}$ to g	Baritone	Low tones ragged. Likely to become a low baritone.
January	122	5′ 8¾″	A youth. Has started to shave.	Husky baritone timbre.	$f_{\prime}$ to $c^{\prime}$♯	$g_{\prime}$ to b♭	Baritone	Break has bothered him for six weeks. Voice skipped an octave.
A year later	132	5′ 10″	More mature looking. Blemishes on face worry him.	Likely to be a low baritone.	$e_{\prime}$ to $d^{\prime}$	$g_{\prime}$ to b	Baritone	The break still occurs, but he has been interested in noting it, and he seems to enjoy being tested.

Case C: A Problem in Adolescent Psychology

Class 7B—Age at First Test: 12 years, 6 months

Studied violin for six months. Sang in grade choir.

Family: American-French. All of the family, large in number, have tried to play an instrument at some time, and all have sung in choirs at school. None of them, however, is especially gifted.

Date of Test	Weight	Height	Physical Appearance	Speaking Voice	Full Range	Comfortable Range	Classification	Remarks
November	172	5′ 8½″	Quite mature. Down on face.	Baritone	$f_{\mid}$ to $E^{\mid}$ with gap of an octave between c and $c^{\mid}$	C to $E^{\mid}$	Soprano I	Always a break singing up or down, and in a descending scale there was a gap of an octave.
End of first semester	182	5′ 9″	So well developed that increase in height and weight hardly noticeable.	Baritone	$e_{\mid}$ to $D^{\mid}$ with gap from c to $c^{\mid}$	D to $D^{\mid}$	Soprano II	Still cannot pass from changed to boy voice without gap of an octave.
Two months later	192	5′ 9″	Looks heavy. Hair on lip noticeable.	Baritone	$e_{\mid}$ to $d^{\mid}$	$f_{\mid}$ to $c^{\mid}$	Low Baritone	Still has gap of an octave.
End of second semester	185	5′ 10″	Boyish expression, but mature physique.	Baritone	$d_{\mid}$ to $D^{\mid}$	$g_{\mid}$ to b	Baritone	Good attitude even in his difficulties.
End of first semester in Grade 8	202	5′ 10½″	Very proud of his physique. Likes to act "tough," but is not really tough.	Baritone of nice quality	$d_{\mid}$ to $D^{\mid}$	$e_{\mid}$ to b	Baritone	Has become very interested in the tests, especially in trying to cover up the break. Passing to falsetto uncomfortable.

Case D: The Sudden Change in the Average Untrained Voice

Class 7B—Age at First Test: 13 years, 10 months

Studied guitar for one year. Sings in school choir.

Family: Interested in music, but neither father nor mother especially gifted; both had played piano.

Date of Test	Weight	Height	Physical Appearance	Speaking Voice	Full Range	Comfortable Range	Classification	Remarks
End of June	128	5′ 4″	Signs of development and growth.	Very husky; spoke as if whispering.	a| to F|#	d to b	Baritone	A little fellow with a nice attitude. Strong desire to grow up.
Mid-October	131	5′ 8″	Has lost his childish looks.	Alto-tenor rather than changed.	a| to a	d to a	Baritone	Almost impossible to get any tone except when well warmed up. Above the break, could not find any voice.
End of November	136	5′ 8¼″	Looks taller; face older looking. Down on lip.	Husky baritone.	a| to a	b|♭ to g	Baritone	After five attempts he could not find his falsetto voice.
End of first semester	136	5′ 8¼″	Youth; blemishes on face.	Baritone.	a|♭ to B	a| to a	Baritone	Found his falsetto voice, and managed quite well at the first attempt. Has lost interest in music because of "gym" activities.

¼″ in height during the semester. During the twelve months following, his growth was ten pounds in weight, 1¼″ in height, and his voice had almost settled. Note that (*1*) the boy voice disappeared during the summer vacation, and (*2*) as new notes developed in the lower range, new notes in the upper range were developing, but slowly. These things can be related to the difficulty the boy had with the break and the gap (as recorded in the remarks) as well as to the spurt in his weight-growth.

As to the boy's attitude towards his voice while he was having difficulty with the break, the report was: "He chose music as an elective because he thought it the smart thing to do. He is an exceptionally fine boy, intelligent, and upright. He became more interested in singing once he saw the reason for the testing."

The progress of this boy's voice is typical of the boy who is not especially talented and whose voice becomes bass. It was reported that he was getting real pleasure from singing, and that although he had a certain poise, he continued to be shy.

CASE C

For a boy not quite thirteen years old, Case C's physique was much above the average. At the first test he was singing Soprano I because he wanted to, but he could have been classified as baritone. Had he been in a grade higher, his attitude might have been very different. During the second semester when it was discovered he was "content to sing in his changed voice," he was classified as baritone. The boy voice had not disappeared as the third test seems to show, for at later tests he had almost the boy voice range he had in the early tests. Had he been a choir boy, at this stage he could have been used as a counter-tenor.

Because there was a gap of an octave in every test while he was in the first semester of Grade 7, I asked about his attitude. The report at the end of the first semester was: "He seems much more settled in his behavior as well as his voice. He is athletic, of the football type; but he still has an immature look. He has been keeping his family in 'hot water.' He is big, husky, and has great strength; has an IQ of 115; is not a disciplinary problem; and does good work. He is content to sing in his changed voice, which he finds more comfortable than the falsetto. He has now adjusted himself to the class and to his surroundings."

By the third test (a period of five months) he had gained twenty pounds; then he lost seven pounds during the next two months, and during the six months following he gained seventeen—evidence of his physiological growth which should be related to his voice development.

At the last test (the end of the first semester in Grade 8) the report was: "He is filling out; is a big husky. Now that others around him have grown up, he does not look so over-sized. I think he has been trying to shave; he has blemishes on his face, and he has lost the awkwardness he had." I was informed that the boy had two brothers to pattern after; they worked for their father, a lake captain, as deck hands during the summer. This may explain his change in attitude during the second semester in Grade 7, when he was becoming adjusted to the new conditions of a junior high school.

CASE D

The fact that Case D could not find his falsetto voice after the summer vacation, that he found it difficult to get any tone at the November test, and that his speaking voice was described as husky, indicate that the change had been a sudden one. Possibly his desire to grow up may have had something to do with his not being able to find his falsetto voice. His attitude was given as "good," so it was not a question of attitude. That he was able to find his falsetto voice at the end of the semester, his teacher ascribes to the intelligent attempts he made.

At the time of the first test, his full range implied that the voice had just changed. The disappearance of the boy voice after the summer vacation was no doubt owing to his not having sung for some time. The disappearance was temporary, for he found his falsetto by the end of the semester.

Note that at the first test the changed voice seemed to have lowered to its limit; also that during the semester after the summer vacation, no new notes developed in the upper range of his changed voice. The boy's interest in "gym" activities rather than music evidently brought about a change in his attitude towards testing, with the result that he did not feel inclined to make as good attempts as he might otherwise have made in helping the upper range of his changed voice to develop.

Part Two

· 10 ·

The Junior High School Boys' Glee Club: Adapting the Alto-Tenor Plan

The alto-tenor classification has made it possible to use four-part music for mixed voices in the junior high school. The workability of this plan is due in large measure to the fact that the tenor part keeps within the alto-tenor range. That so much music for soprano, alto, alto-tenor, and bass is available in America today is evidence of the demand for it and proof of its practical value for junior high school purposes. Four-part music of this type suits the voice conditions of the entire junior high school, with the exception of those seventh grade classes which have no alto-tenors. If there are changed voices in a seventh grade class, there is no alternative but to use music for soprano, alto, and bass. This three-part music, however, is not suitable for eighth and ninth grades in which many voices reach the alto-tenor stage.

As few schools have separate classes for boys and girls, the alto-tenor plan has been worked out in terms of mixed classes. During the last two or three decades, however, the movement towards the junior high school boys' glee club has gained in momentum and popularity, and this seems to be putting a new complexion on the alto-tenor plan. There are few schools which today do not have a boys' glee club, either elective or extracurricular.

The junior high school boys' glee club is an offshoot of the high school boys' glee club, which, in turn, was patterned after the adult male voice glee club. When the boys' glee club began to make its appearance in the junior high school around 1920, it was an extracurricular activity intended for selected students. At that time it was regarded as a junior grade of the high school club, having the same voice classifications and therefore using the same type of music. The requirements included not only talent, but voices that would fit the classifications of the high school glee club. However, as the junior high school boys' glee club became an elective and was given a place in the curriculum, its scope was widened so that boys with voices in the early adolescent stage were eligible. Boys with a second soprano range could be accepted, whereas hitherto there was no place for them. (This explains the longer ranges for Tenor I in Examples 3, 4, 5, and 6, on page 80.) The elective glee club is in line with the philosophy of the junior high school in that it takes note of the pupils' inclinations. It is possible to program the boys' glee club as an elective because of the music that has been provided to suit its voice conditions, the so-called T.T.B.B. arrangement.

THE T.T.B.B. CLASSIFICATION

The T.T.B.B. classification of the junior high school boys' glee club has been ridiculed by many musicians who are not conversant with junior high school work and its aims. They cannot understand, for example, why a boy whose voice is Soprano II or Alto should be called Tenor I in the boys' glee club. As far as the boy is concerned, he prefers to be called Tenor I in the glee club, even though he knows he does not have a tenor voice. Similarly, the boy classified as Bass I in the boys' glee club, and alto-tenor in class, knows his voice is not bass; but he prefers to be called bass in a boys' group.

A criticism that can well be made of the alto-tenor classification is that although it suits the slowly changing type of voice, it does not suit the quickly changing type nearly so well, and the latter type is always more numerous in any group of junior high school boys. At a certain stage, the boy whose voice is changing quickly has difficulty in singing the alto-tenor part in the music texts compiled for mixed voice work. This stage occurs when the comfortable range has lowered one or two tones below the accepted alto-tenor range. The voice is not classifiable as bass because its comfortable range is approximately e to d' (bass), and it does not remain long at this stage. The boy feels this lower range is more comfortable and easier to manage than the alto-tenor one. The T.T.B.B. classification of the boys' glee club suits this voice, which is classified as Bass I.

MUSIC COLLECTIONS FOR THE BOYS' GLEE CLUB

An examination of the collections in use today shows that the accepted alto-tenor range is seldom used, but that one a little higher and another a little lower take care of what is in essence an alto-tenor part.

The Chorus Book for Boys, by Ella M. Probst and J. Victor Berquist (2 vols., New York, G. Schirmer, 1922 and 1925), is the pioneer collection for junior high school boys' glee clubs.[1] T. P. Giddings supplies a

[1] A revised edition of this collection (now out of print) was issued in one volume in 1932 under the title *Junior Gleemen,* with a preface by Louis Woodson Curtis, Director of Music, Los Angeles Schools, at the time. Unfortunately, the foreword by Mr. Giddings has been omitted.

foreword in which he says: "The number of boys' classes in the junior high school and the popularity of boys' glee clubs in the seventh, eighth, and ninth grades have created a demand for music to fit the boy voice at this age. The safe and easy compass of the boy voice in these grades is very limited and the music in these books has been arranged specially with this fact in mind. Boys' voices in these grades fall into six divisions—first and second soprano, first and second alto, first and second bass. Very rarely will there be found a tenor, as this voice develops later. Very few first sopranos and comparatively few second sopranos will be found, for the voices of nearly all the boys have begun to change, and this means that only the middle and lower parts of the voice should be used, no matter how big and brilliant the upper tones may be." The ranges and classifications are given in Example 1.

It would be difficult to find a boy whose voice did not fit into one of the categories named. The only comment might be on "a few basses with a high range," included under Bass I. In Volume II the range for this voice is given as f to e' flat (bass). I asked Mary H. Kiess, Haven School, Evanston, Illinois (whose junior high school boys' glee club made such a favorable impression at the Music Educators Conference, Milwaukee, Wisconsin, in 1942), if she would comment on this. She replied: "In my group I had two boys singing the Bass I part whose voices would test as baritones. From the tone quality I believe they will later on develop into tenors. They are more mature than the other boys; one has a low IQ and the other is a colored boy who is vocally older than most in the group. I imagine Mr. Giddings refers to such cases. These boys give a solidity to the Bass I section, which is generally needed, and I think it well for them to be giving their upper tones a chance. Both of these boys sing the bass part in my mixed voice group."

The Glenn Glee Club Book for Boys, by Mabelle Glenn and Virginia French (New York, Oliver Ditson, 1927), a collection which has been very widely used, was "compiled to meet the need of material for boys' choruses, though many of the selections will be found interesting for mixed classes in the junior high school." In the preface to the book, Dr. Glenn gives her views on the boy voice question. "The voices of boys of junior high school age fall into four divisions—soprano, alto, alto-tenor, and bass. The increasing care which is being given to the head voice in the grade schools, brings a larger number of boys with soprano voices into the junior high school. The boy who has a clear, liquid voice and who has carried with him into the junior high school an ideal of unforced, floating head tone, is perfectly safe on the soprano part. However, a much larger number fit into the alto part. Usually for four or five months before a boy's voice changes, the tones from G above middle C to G below middle C are most beautiful and round. Boys in this limited range are called alto-tenors. . . . As a rule all changed voices in the junior high school should sing the bass part. It is most unusual to find a changed voice which is safe on the tenor part. In this book the bass part is kept in an easy, safe range. Teachers should watch the change in every boy's voice and with the first indication of the voice lowering, should transfer the boy to a lower part, regardless of the balance of parts in the chorus."

Criticism has been made that the alto-tenor parts in this collection are too high. To determine whether this criticism is just or not, the following points should be taken into consideration: (*1*) The junior high school period in Kansas City, Missouri, where Dr. Glenn was Director of Music for many years, is two years. (*2*) In the Kansas City junior high schools, boys' music classes are separate from girls'. (*3*) Boys entering the junior high schools from the grade schools of the city have been trained to sing with "unforced, floating head tone," and they can also read music fluently.

Because the junior high school period in Kansas City is two years, the book is intended to suit the boy voice conditions only through the seventh and eighth grades. Because the boys' classes are separate, there is no need to put altos in the alto-tenor section too soon, as is done so often in mixed classes to get balance of some kind for four-part music. Dr. Glenn speaks of the "beautiful and round" tone of the boy's voice four or five months before it begins to change. This kind of tone is heard only if the previous training has made it possible. Unfortunately, it is heard in very few schools. Raucous tone seems to be the characteristic of the boy voice at this stage in many schools, and it is from these schools that criticism about the highness of the alto-tenor part might come.

The preface of *Twice 55 Part Songs for Boys: The Orange Book* (Boston, Birchard, 1927) states: "Any group of boys between the ages of 11 and 15 will usually include soprano voices which apparently are pure treble; bass voices which have much of the range, if not the full quality, of a mature male voice; and several voices in between these two extremes—alto, alto-tenor, tenor, and baritone. The inner voices during the period of change have very narrow ranges, and usually the low voices do best when they have a restricted range. This collection not only seeks to meet these needs, but in doing so, to give that characteristic full, even, close harmony effect which is the charm of male voice music. . . . The aim has been to keep each part within the range of an octave or less. Higher or lower notes occasionally occur, but the majority of the songs conform to these limits and in many cases to even narrower ones." The ranges are shown in Example 2.

A criticism that has been made of the music in this book is that it is not effective with junior high school boys because it is too low; that if it is transposed up, say, a tone, the lower parts are put out of their comfortable ranges. It may be noted that the book was published in the same year as the Glenn book, in the days when boys' glee clubs (junior high as well as high school) were practically all extracurricular. Since the voices were selected, generally only those which conformed to the ranges of the book were chosen. If the music was too low to be effective for these voices, one can only assume that forcing was used to get the effect of the adult male voice glee club to some extent. Therefore, the tone was not pleasant.

It is difficult to agree with the criticism made about the book. If the proper quality of tone, in terms of a boys' glee club, is sought from each section and is obtained, the effect will be musical and pleasant to listen to; but it should be kept in mind that the tonal results possible from a junior high school glee club singing in the ranges in this book are quite different from those possible in a high school glee club. It is not the arrangements that are at fault, but a misconception of what is possible from a junior high school boys' glee club.

The collections to be considered next were published ten years or more later than those just examined. Boys in the early adolescent stage—that is, from the Soprano II stage—are now taken into glee clubs, as is evident from the fact that provision is made for them in the Tenor I classification.

In the foreword to *When Voices are Changing* by William Breach (Philadelphia, Presser, 1936), Mr. Breach says of the alto classification: "When the boy can sing easily in the range F (below middle C) to C' (octave above middle C) in a mixed voice chorus, he should be classified as alto. In the adolescent boys' glee club, we should use him for the highest part, and in order to parallel the adult male chorus, we call him Tenor I." The ranges and classifications are shown in Example 3. Mr. Breach offers two suggestions that, if followed, do much to improve the boys' glee club singing: (*1*) Avoid chesty singing; it is highly essential that the adolescent voice be used lightly and that it be coaxed into the lower range. (*2*) Do not strive for brilliant effects with the adolescent boys' glee club; there is a temptation to work for a body of tone comparable to that possible with an adult male glee club. Such a procedure will cause the voices to strain and will defeat the object of bringing the boy voice down gradually and easily into the changed voice. It is a better plan to work for beautiful tone quality, fine blend of voices, and careful diction.

Mr. Breach speaks of the necessity of "crystallizing the voices of each section once they have been tested and classified for the glee clubs." By this is meant "to make each boy conscious of the voice range to be sung by his section and to unify the voice in each section." This is accomplished by using "vocal exercises an octave or less in compass in such keys as are necessary to keep each section within the proper range. Unison songs of limited compass may also be used in this way."

In this connection, Jacob Evanston, Supervisor of Choral Music, Pittsburgh, Pennsylvania, advocates more unison singing in both the junior high and the high school. He says: "We must never leave out unison singing; it is basic in all choral work for groups at all ages. In the junior and senior high school unison singing is a lost art. Consider what the choral speech teachers, such as Marjorie Gullan, for instance, are doing. They have stolen our thunder and left the best part out—the tune. My experience in Pittsburgh has given me the perspective to see that we have exaggerated the complex in music. This has defeated our efforts at every level, except in the hands of the exceptional teacher. Voice production in part-singing is in no way so very different from voice production in solo singing. The teacher should shy away from using complex music constantly, that is, in respect to the number of parts. Other things being equal, it seems to me as though it is twice as hard to sing in two parts as it is in one, twice as hard in three parts as in two, and so on. Many of our tonal problems, especially with adolescent boys, would be fewer if we gave the alto and alto-tenor sections some unison work, provided the teacher has the right feeling for the naturally resonant, naturally intense, and naturally controlled tone which is possible at these stages."

Four-Part Songs for Junior High School Boys, by Ralph Wright and William Lester (Chicago, Gamble Hinged Music Co., 1936) shows another way of naming the voice classifications for adolescent boys. (See Example 4.) "The ability of boys should not be underestimated," says Mr. Wright in the foreword. "Boys can sing music which is difficult if they are musical and if it is within their vocal range."

Glee Music for Junior High School Boys, by Robert W. Gibbs and Haydn Morgan (Boston, Birchard, 1937) has as a subtitle, "For Unchanged, Changing, and Changed Voices." Of the forty-nine numbers in the book, four are unison, five are three-part for S.A.B., and the remainder are four-part. The compilers of this book state that it is intended for all stages of advancement (from unison and simple three-part songs for newly organized clubs to more elaborate four-part program selections for more advanced organizations) and that the arrangements have been made with special care to give the close harmony effect found in music for male voices. The voice classifications and ranges are shown in Example 5.

This book is the first one to include unison songs, though Mr. Breach in *When Voices are Changing* takes note of the unison song for voice training purposes. On the other hand, Mr. Wright in *Four-Part Songs for Junior High School Boys* says: "Boys in the junior high cannot sing unison songs satisfactorily because of the limited range of their voices." It depends on what is meant by "satisfactorily," and on the teacher's idea of what is possible. The unison song is much to be preferred to the vocal exercise for voice training purposes.

Troubadors: A Collection of Four-Part Choruses by Mae Nightingale (New York, Carl Fischer, 1939) was prepared for the schools of Los Angeles. Because there had been a general criticism that the alto-tenor parts of the music books prepared by eastern editors were too high for California boys, a committee of music teachers of the junior and senior high schools of Los Angeles specified the voice ranges that should be used in this collection. (See Example 6.)

According to the preface, *Troubadors* is designed as a basic text to meet the vocal requirements of adolesecent boys' four-part organizations in any stage of musical development, or of those mixed groups with limited range, providing for a gradual transition from the elementary grades to the advanced work in the senior high school. "The four-part arrangements are so planned that all parts lie well within a range which allows for transposition up or down when necessary. By using the easiest and most comfortable part of the range, the student's voice is put to the least possible strain. Careful attention has been given to the alto-tenor or changing voice, thus preserving the voice quality and making it possible for the boy to continue singing even though his range may be limited to a few tones. . . . Alternate notes have been indicated to provide for the slight variation in range and voice quality that occurs in all groups from year to year. . . . In several instances the alternate notes are preferable from a musical standpoint, but may not be possible because of range limitations."

T.T.B.B. AND THE ALTO-TENOR PLAN

In none of the foregoing collections does the alto-tenor range appear. Instead, there is one a little higher, which is suitable for the pre-alto-tenor stage, and one a little lower, which is suitable for the post-alto-tenor stage. The classifications for these stages have been named Tenor II for the former, and Bass I for the latter. The Tenor II classification suits all changing voices just before the mutation begins, and Bass I after it has started, particularly the quickly changing voices. Classified as Tenor II, the boy has not begun to encounter difficulties of voice control, whereas classified as Bass I, he has, but not to the same degree as if he were singing an alto-tenor part. The Bass I range, too, is more practical than the alto-tenor one for the quickly changing type of voice, and because these voices are always more numerous than the slowly changing, it would seem that the alto-tenor plan might well be modified. The boys'

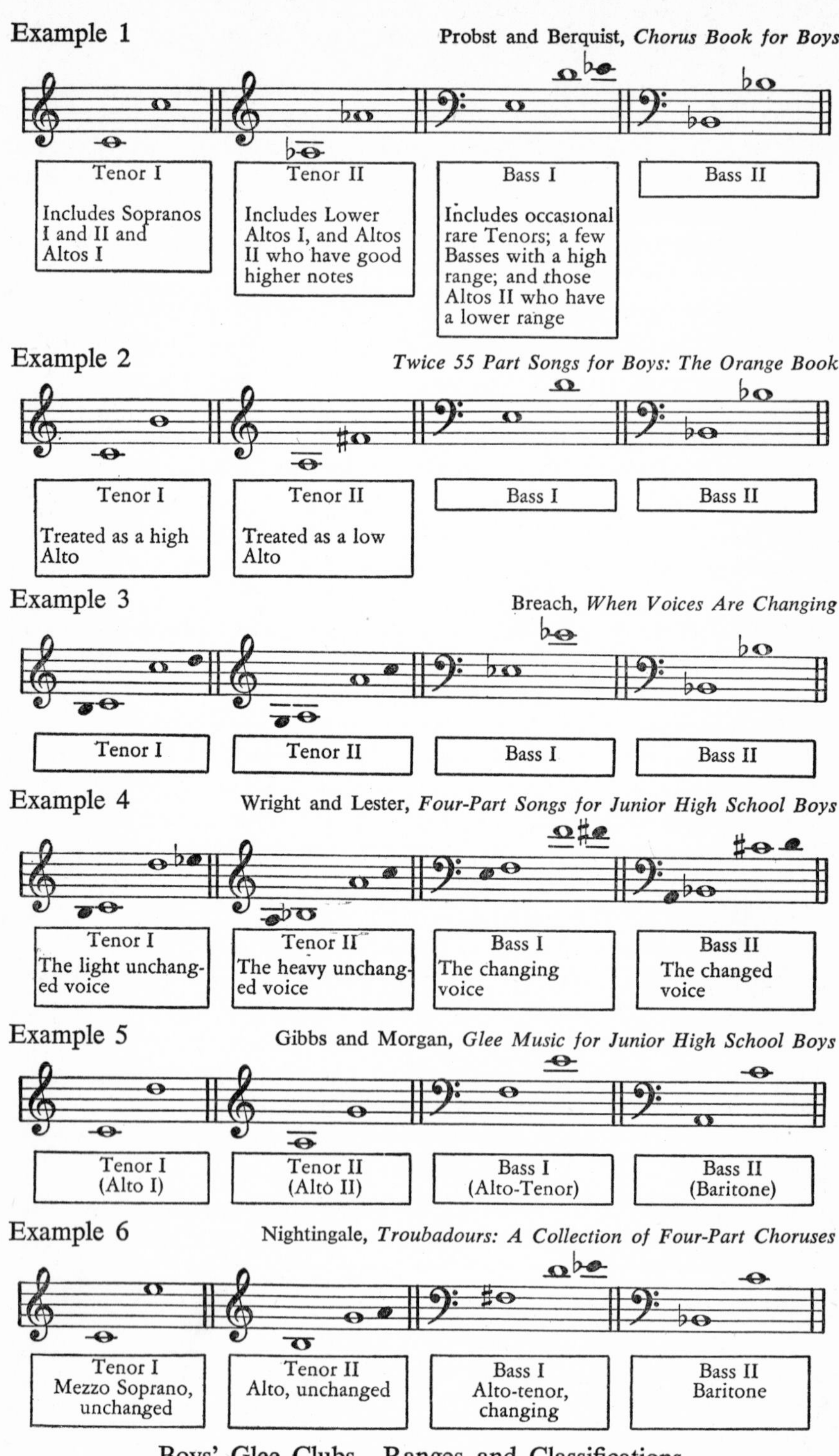

Boys' Glee Clubs—Ranges and Classifications

glee club and its plan of classification imply the need for an adaptation of the alto-tenor plan. If it were modified, however, a problem would arise in mixed voice work, that of classifying quickly changing voices at the Bass I stage of the boys' glee club. These voices could not be classified as bass unless there were some kind of "baritone" classification.

Two questions might well be asked: Why have boys' glee clubs become so numerous and so popular? And why, after years of experimentation with the alto-tenor plan, are mixed choruses not more numerous than they are in the junior high school? Quite apart from the psychological aspect of the matter, have not the range specifications of the more recently published collections for boys' glee clubs been a factor in making boys' glee clubs popular? The alto-tenor section of the mixed chorus has been, and always will be, a problem. It does not remain intact for any length of time; but neither does the Bass I section of the boys' glee club. The vocal problems, however, are not so troublesome in the Bass I classification for the majority of boys, and so they find it more enjoyable to sing in this range than in the alto-tenor range.

The T.T.B.B. classification of the boys' glee club is really a modified mixed voice classification, in which the Tenor I part could be for Soprano I (if any) and Soprano II; the Tenor II part for Altos and high Alto-Tenors; the Bass I part for low Alto-Tenors and Baritones with a short range; and the Bass II part for Basses. It would seem, therefore, that for mixed voice work the present alto-tenor classification would have to be subdivided into Alto-Tenor I and II. Thus instead of four-part music, it would be necessary to have five-part: Soprano, Alto, Alto-Tenor I, Alto-Tenor II, and Bass.

In sum, the T.T.B.B. classification of the junior high school boys' glee club suits the voice conditions of a group of adolescent boys. In a mixed junior high school chorus the alto-tenor plan suits the slowly, and slower, changing voices better than the quickly changing. With the latter the principles of the baritone plan might be followed for the time being. No one plan suits every boy's voice, whether in the boys' glee club or the mixed chorus, and it is a mistake to try to make one plan fit.

THE CAMBIATA PLAN

Dr. Irvin Cooper, Professor of Music Education, Florida State University, has an idea akin to the writer's that the alto-tenor plan needs some modification. In his song book for junior high schools, *Tunetime for Teentime* (New York, Carl Fischer, 1952),[2] he uses the term "cambiata"

[2] The subtitle states that the book is "a selection of songs compiled and arranged in melody-style, in unison, two-part, and four-part, for Unchanged (girl or boy), Changing (Cambiata), and Changed (light baritone) voices."

(from *nota cambiata,* changing note in counterpoint) instead of alto-tenor for the boy's changing voice and the part he sings, the third part of four-part music for mixed voices. In the foreword to the book, he says: "The designation of the changing voice as 'cambiata' is to avoid confusion with the frequent misconception attending the scope of the alto-tenor range. Recognition and classification of the 'cambiata' voice is one of the greatest problems of the junior high school teacher, because, owing to its most unusual timbre, it is often mistaken for a baritone due to an aural illusion of singing an octave lower than it actually sings. If the teacher tries to identify cambiata by individual testing, the result will be negative, as it is only discernible when tested in company with other, better known vocal types."

The classification of voices, with their ranges, used in *Tunetime for Teentime* is as follows: Soprano, $B_{,}$ flat to F', treble staff (*tessitura* D to D'); Cambiata, $A_{,}$ to C', treble staff (*tessitura* $A_{,}$ to A); Baritone, $B_{,}$ flat to F', bass staff (*tessitura* C to C'); and rarely, Bass, $F_{,}$ to C'. For unison singing by all voices, the range is $B_{,}$ flat to C'. The method of classification is to use a known song, the compass of which lies within B flat and its octave above. The whole class sings the song. Obviously each pupil will use the voice that is natural to him and in his comfortable range; that is, some will sing in the lower octave and others in the higher. The teacher moves among the boys as quickly as possible, tapping those who are singing in the lower octave; these are the baritones, and they are told to be silent for the remainder of the test. The class, except the baritones, sings the song again, but in a key a fifth to a sixth higher. Those boys who have soprano voices are tapped and are asked to be silent after being tapped. The remainder of the boys, the untapped ones, are the cambiata group. It is then recommended that the song be sung in the lower key by the cambiata group only, so that the teacher and the boys will have a mental concept of the tone of a group of cambiata voices.

The song book is "so organized that the various numbers may be sung as unison songs for girls', boys' or mixed voices, as well as in parts for boys' or mixed voices." Under the title of each number the various voice arrangements that are possible are given, thus: Part I (Soprano), Part II (Soprano), Part III (Cambiata), Part IV (Baritone), the key being that of the printed music. If the song can be used by boys' voices only (boys' glee clubs) by transposing it, it is indicated thus: Part I (Cambiata), Part II (Cambiata), Part III (Baritone), Part IV (Baritone or occasionally Bass). If the number can also be used as a unison song, the key is stated. Most of the numbers are of this type, that is, they are for mixed voices, or by transposition for boys' glee clubs, or for unison for all voices in the key stated.

The concluding paragraph of the foreword, which calls for some comment, reads as follows: "By a thoughtful understanding of the working area of boys' voices during the changing period and a use of material within the limits of these voices, a choral teacher can preserve potential tenors. . . . Conversely, by carelessly exposing all the boys to songs which are in the baritone range, potential tenors either become indifferent baritones or drop out of singing altogether. In either case the scarcity of tenors remains in *status quo*."

The cambiata plan [3] is one that is very suitable for potential tenors insofar as they are slowly changing or slower changing voices; and a cambiata will be classified as tenor when his voice has lowered to the tenor range. The quickly changing voices, however, will give evidence at certain stages that they are not going to develop to tenor, but to baritone or bass, and they will have to be transferred to baritone when they are no longer able to sing the cambiata part. The question is: What are the criteria in determining when the transfer should be made? Dr. Cooper does not make this clear. In an article, "The Junior High School Choral Problem," he says: "Following the cambiata period the subsequent progress towards the boy's vocal maturity is either to tenor or light baritone, which rests between low B flat and high F (bass staff). This is rarely understood thoroughly, because tradition insists that high F is too high for the average baritone." [4]

When a cambiata is transferred to baritone, no matter what his range is, he will sing in one that is comfortable to him (as happens in any plan), and in time—sooner for some than others—the voice will have dropped to the baritone range. If the light baritone range is that given by Dr. Cooper, keeping in mind that boys of junior high school age are being considered, what is the timbre of the upper notes? Is it cambiata or boy baritone? Is there a difference between the timbres? A boy can sing high F if he has been trained to use his falsetto voice, and can pass from the changed to the falsetto without a break. Otherwise, is it not better to restrict the baritone range to the *tessitura* one of D to D' and allow the baritone voice to develop during the junior high school period, and as it matures during the high school period to cultivate the falsetto with a view to its developing into the higher notes of the baritone range?

[3] The plan is described in Irvin Cooper's *Letters to Pat* (New York, Carl Fischer, 1953).

[4] *Music Educators Journal* (Chicago), November-December, 1950.

· 11 ·

The Adolescent Boy in the American Church Choir Program

One of the chief problems of the senior choir of mixed voices in churches is that of keeping up the men's sections. To meet the problem there must be a definite plan to ensure a steady supply of young men trained to fill vacancies in the tenor and bass sections.

Formerly, the choirmaster considered his work to be the preparation of the Sunday music by the senior choir and the organization of a junior choir for special occasions. The progressive choirmaster, on the other hand, realized that there was a missing link in the work, namely, the lack of interest in the boy's voice during the adolescent period. Hitherto, the attitude was: Why bother about the boy's voice during this period as it is of no use for choir purposes? Consequently, no attempt was made to bridge the gap between the junior and the senior choir as far as the boy was concerned. The loss of potentially good material for the male sections of the senior choir has been considerable. In view of what is being done with boys' voices in the junior high and high schools, it is surprising that so few choirmasters have made use of the music instruction given in these schools.

In this chapter are described three plans that choirmasters have worked out to keep boys of the junior choirs interested in choir work during the adolescent period, with a view to preparing them to take their places in the senior choir as soon as they are ready.

THE MULTIPLE CHOIR PLAN

"In order that an adult volunteer choir may thrive and develop over a period of years, it seems that the best thing to do is to build a succession of younger choirs so that there will be a continual supply of material coming up. The system of choirs should be a logical and normal development that serves the membership of the church in all its departments; that is to say, the plan must fit the church program rather than the reverse, in order to accommodate the choirs. The choirmaster must have a long range view and a clear picture of the entire program of the church to judge what is needed. Multiple choirs do not fit all churches, but they can for most. In my church we are organized on what is termed the five-year plan."[1] This is the conception that Donald C. Gilley had of his work while he was Minister of Music at Wesley Methodist Church, Worcester, Massachusetts, from 1938 to 1942. His five-choir plan, based on the work of his predecessor, Arthur Leslie Jacobs, is as follows:

1) Boys' Choir; ages 8 to 12. One rehearsal of one hour a week.
2) Girls' Choir; ages 8 to 12. One rehearsal of one hour a week.
3) Vesper Choir of Boys and Girls; ages 12 to 16 or 17. One rehearsal of one hour a week.
4) Chapel Choir of Mixed Voices; ages 17 to 21. A two-hour rehearsal weekly.
5) Senior Choir. A two-hour rehearsal weekly.

One season the children's choirs of his church numbered about sixty-five boys and girls; the Vesper Choir, fifty-five; the Chapel Choir, forty-three; and the Senior Choir, fifty-four. The Chapel and the Senior Choirs combined for the Sunday services and were limited to one hundred because of the seating accommodation. "It would be impossible to carry on these older choirs were it not for the younger groups," said Mr. Gilley. "That the plan is sound, I can verify from experience. Both choir and members have benefited by the system, and musical as well as spiritual gains have been made."

It is in the Vesper Choir that boys with changing voices are found. "To organize a choir of this kind, by all means keep the boys with changing voices," said Mr. Gilley. "They can be used if their problems are studied; they are not of any great help, but they will be later on. If they are used in the public schools, why cannot we use them in the church? The music for this group, however, must be chosen very carefully. I find unison music and descants ideal. The vocal range must be moderate and ought not at any time to be such as to produce strain. Careful vocalization is necessary, with special attention to the boys. . . . Let the boys understand that the notes which are out of their range are not to be sung—and these will be different from rehearsal to rehearsal. Even if a boy is able to sing only a few notes, the rehearsal work still has a value for him. Bear with these boys and they will be useful later on." Two-part music (S.A.) was used only occasionally as there was not sufficient time for the preparation of more than an occasional number. The older boys who would be classified as alto-tenor were called alto by Mr. Gilley, as he had

[1] D. C. Gilley, "Handling Problems, Administrative and Choral, in Choir Work," a paper read at the convention of the American Guild of Organists in Washington, D. C., in June 1941. (Published in *Diapason* [Chicago], September 1941.)

no need to use the alto-tenor classification. However, he used vocalization exercises in the alto-tenor range (downward exercises of five notes scalewise) as a preparation to help the boy later on. He preferred, he said, to let the music being learned take care of the lowering of the voices.

In the Vesper Choir the aim was to have as many boys as possible, so that in their late teens some would be ready for the Chapel Choir. Usually, the majority of the alto boys were from twelve to fourteen years of age and likely to become basses. Boys over fourteen, who were in the minority, included those with slowly changing voices, the potential tenors. "It is rather unusual for a boy to come immediately into the tenor section of the Chapel Choir upon his voice having finished the first major change. I have in my own mind almost made it a rule to start the youngest boys, who have just finished the first major change, in the baritone section, even though I think they are going to become tenors. One can usually tell, but not always. They need training to know how to use their voices in the upper register, and I prefer that they learn to sing easily in the middle register before working in the extremes."

Because he was conversant with what was being done in the junior high school, I asked Mr. Gilley what his views were on three questions: (*1*) Would you keep a boy in the Vesper Choir if his changed voice had developed a range of B flat to the octave above (bass clef) and he could still sing alto in a limited compass? (*2*) Would you transfer to the Chapel Choir boys of fourteen and fifteen years whose voices had changed to bass, provided they had a comfortable range of approximately an octave? (*3*) What is your attitude if the boy wants to sing in his changed voice rather than in his boy voice? Mr. Gilley replied as follows: "I try to make a boy as comfortable as possible vocally, no matter at what stage his voice is. There are social as well as musical reasons which have to be taken into consideration. I do not like to take a boy into the Chapel Choir until he has passed the fifteen-year mark, because he just does not fit into the group. As a rule, it does not injure his voice to use the portion that is left at the upper end in all the singing he does in the Vesper Choir, and unless I encounter strenuous resistance, I let him remain in the Vesper Choir. This means, of course, that he is not a particularly useful member of the choir, because his range is short. I do not try to develop countertenors as Father Finn does, for example, but rather let nature takes its course by having the boy use gently, and as freely as possible, what little voice he may have during this period. I have noticed that the boys do not seem self-conscious, because they have the same situation in school, of not being able to enter fully into all the singing that is done. My procedure is determined by trying to avoid making the boy do anything that will be injurious to his voice through hastening the work that nature is doing.

I lose some boys whose voices change around fourteen, but more because of lack of interest than because of voice problems. It must be remembered that my only hold on these boys is their interest. However, I can usually pick them up again when their voices have changed sufficiently and admit them to the Chapel Choir."

In his paper, Mr. Gilley made some apt remarks about the tone quality of choirs, for example: "Remember your junior choir is not an Episcopal boy choir, and do not try to imitate its tone quality. The junior choir has its own contribution to make, and its function is not that of imitation." Another remark, while applicable to any choir, is especially pertinent to choirs of the type of his Vesper and Chapel choirs: "The tone quality of any choir is not static; it changes suddenly. . . . Be thankful for this, for as it changes, it can be changed for the better."

THE YOUNG MEN'S ENSEMBLE

Arthur Leslie Jacobs, while he was Minister of Music in the First Congregational Church of Los Angeles, established another five-choir plan: the Cathedral Choir, the Church of Youth Choir, the High School Choir, the Children's Choir, and the Boys' Choir. Each choir sang at its own regular Sunday service. In addition, as part of the music program of the church, there was a Young Men's Ensemble, an Adult Orchestra, and a Children's Orchestra.[2]

Mr. Jacobs expressed his attitude towards the adolescent boy in relation to choir work in the following statement: "The adolescent boy is an interesting problem. In general, so far as musical results are concerned, work with him is not very satisfactory. However, I use adolescent boys in my plan for the sake of the boys themselves. Accordingly, I have a Young Men's Ensemble, which is meant to take care of those boys who are no

[2] Mr. Jacobs was formerly at Wesley Church, Worcester, Massachusetts, where he originated and worked out the multiple-choir plan that Mr. Gilley carried on; but Mr. Jacobs modified it by adding the Young Men's Ensemble. In 1946, he gave up his position in the First Congregational Church of Los Angeles to become Director of the Department of Music for the Church Federation of Los Angeles and the Southern Council of Protestant Churches. He resigned from this position in 1951.

The Church of Youth was organized to meet the needs and interests of young people of eighteen to thirty years; it had its own minister, choir, board of officials, and financial reports. The First Congregational Church of Los Angeles had perhaps one of the most comprehensive music programs in the country. In 1941 the music staff consisted of two assistant directors, two full-time organists, ten volunteer organists, and a secretary. Mrs. Jacobs had charge of all the children's choirs. Mr. Jacobs' duties included the planning and supervision of seven regular Sunday services, two daily week-day services, five choirs each singing its own Sunday services, a Holy Week schedule of eighteen services, a series of Vesper recitals, an annual two-day Bach Festival featuring the Cathedral Choir and the Los Angeles Symphony Orchestra, annual presentations of *The Messiah,* Brahms' *Requiem,* and Haydn's *Passion,* and an annual festival of modern music.

longer able to be in the Boys' Choir, and who are not ready to sing tenor or bass in the High School (Church) Choir. It is so easy to lose boys in this transitional period. The work with this group is therefore definitely a preparation for membership in the High School Choir. The church must save these boys for itself in some manner; music can do it. The members of this group have all been in the children's choirs and have sung alto for different lengths of time. I never let a boy sing alto any longer than I think he reasonably can. The Young Men's Ensemble takes part in services, and although I encourage the boys to sing, I do not expect anything of them vocally. My chief concern is to tide them over vocally and emotionally until they are ready for the High School Choir. They sing what they can of the tenor part."

The plan of dealing with the voices in the Young Men's Ensemble was to have the boys vocalize in a medium range, starting from the lower treble and singing down into the upper man's voice. Because it was difficult to find music to use with them, bass parts which were rather high and tenor parts which were rather low were selected from the repertoire of the senior choirs. In other words the procedure was more or less that used for alto-tenors in school. From its nature the ensemble was not in any sense a choir, and it was never a large group—any number up to eight.

The Young Men's Ensemble is a definite step toward ensuring a supply of young men for the senior choir. The aim with such a group, the weakest group in the multiple choir plan, should be to make it as strong a link as possible between the junior and the senior choirs. Its success depends on the choirmaster's attitude towards it and his philosophy concerning it. A statement of Mr. Jacobs' philosophy towards his work was given in the 1941 *Year Book* of the First Congregational Church of Los Angeles. It starts: "With the amazing growth in recent years of musical culture, churches have begun to develop more fully their music programs. . . . In the church music program people dare not merely listen to music; they must make it, and as many as possible must share in it. The church music experience must start with, and be fostered in, the young child. No amount of over-emphasis can be placed on music training for children in the church program. The complete program, therefore, must include choirs for nearly all ages; and it should have instrumental groups for children and adults, classes in the various phases of music appreciation, programs for pure enjoyment, vesper programs from among the talent of the community. The church dare not stop with the making of Sunday music only, if lives are to be influenced, and if music is to grow under church influence."

THE YOUNG PEOPLE'S CHOIR

During his tenure as Minister of Music at the Church of the Covenant, Erie, Pennsylvania, Dr. Federal Whittlesey [3] established the following multiple choir plan:

1) A Carol Choir for boys and girls; ages 5 to 7. One rehearsal of 45 minutes a week.
2) A Junior Choir for boys and girls; ages 8 to 10. One rehearsal of 45 minutes a week.
3) The Boys' Choir. Two rehearsals a week, one for 45 minutes and the other (on Saturdays) for an hour.
4) The Young People's Choir for young ladies and gentlemen; ages 14 to 17. One rehearsal of 90 minutes a week.
5) The Covenant Choir (the senior choir). One rehearsal a week.

There was also an Oratorio Chorus of fifty voices which joined with the Covenant Choir in presenting *The Messiah* and Haydn's *Creation,* as well as a male chorus of twenty (an activity of the Men's Association of the church) and a string ensemble which was organized to take part in any church activity where it could be used.

"The Young People's Choir is an adult choir, the first of the grown-up units; to develop such a choir, the director must have this hypothesis. If he embraces this theory, it will influence everything he does with this choir. It will effect his selection of singers, the voice work he does with them, the way he handles the group, and the music he uses. Fourteen to seventeen is a critical period. . . . It is during this period that it is particularly necessary for the church to hold her young people. They need the stabilizing influence of church life and worship. It is here that a choir can be of help. There are many young people interested in music, and through the choir they can be retained in the church."

There was no graded choir plan in the Church of the Covenant when Dr. Whittlesey took up his duties there, and he relates that when he went

[3] Since 1949, Dr. Whittlesey has been Minister of Music, Highland Park Methodist Church, Dallas, Texas, where his multiple choir plan is: Carol Choir (boys and girls in the first and second grades); Junior Choir (boys and girls in the third, fourth, and fifth grades); Junior II Girl Choir (girls in the sixth grade); Boy Choir (boys in the fifth through the ninth grades); Girl Choir (girls in the seventh, eighth, and ninth grades); Young People's Choir (young men and women in the tenth, eleventh, and twelfth grades); Chancel Choir (adults of college age and older). These choirs meet weekly throughout most of the year. Dr. Whittlesey first experimented with a graded choir plan while he was at Westminster Church, Detroit, Michigan. Starting with three choirs—one for adults, one for young people, and one for juniors—he divided some of the choirs and added others as the plan developed. The quotations which are given in this section are taken from an article by Dr. Whittlesey in the *Music Teachers Review* (now discontinued), Spring 1942.

about getting members for the Young People's Choir, he approached the "young ladies and gentlemen" personally and directly, making it his business to know the leaders of the youth life in the church, especially the boys. He also sought the help of the high school music supervisor. "The church music director should cultivate the friendship and good will of the high school music teacher of his vicinity. The high schools have developed such fine choirs, it behooves the church musician to know what they are doing. The young people who sing in these choirs will probably be interested in the church choir program of a director who is interested in them, and the high school director will be inclined to send any of his singers who are not members of other churches to a director whom he knows and respects."

It is not surprising to find that Dr. Whittlesey's plan of dealing with boys' voices at the transition stage is akin to the alto-tenor plan of the junior high school. "If there are boys eligible as far as age is concerned, who want to sing in the Young People's Choir, but whose voices have not changed, they can be used. Put them in the tenor section; they will sing in the lower part of their unchanged voice, which is the easy part of the tenor range. The quality will be different from that of the tenors, but this will not do any particular harm. If it is a question of sacrificing the quality slightly or losing the interest of the boy, the former is preferable. As the changed voice develops, the young men will be placed in whichever section they belong once the voice shows it will be tenor or bass." Group voice training is advocated for the Young People's Choir.

Regarding repertoire, Dr. Whittlesey says: "Do not sneer at unison anthems. Better an expressive unison than a labored four-part anthem. It may be advisable to use S.A.B. music if the choir is short of men (that is, boys with changed voices) or if they are not experienced in part-singing." As soon as there is sufficient balance and music development, however, four-part anthems may be recommended.

In the matter of public performance Dr. Whittlesey recognizes the psychological effect it has on young people. "The Young People's Choir will sing more often in public than the children's choir but will not be expected to sing as many services as the adult choir. It should sing often at young people's meetings and other church functions. The members will be greatly stimulated by an occasional visit to another church or an out-of-town trip. Give the young people worthwhile responsibility and they will rise to the occasion. Treat them as grown-ups and they will respond as such. Lavish your efforts on this choir; it is worth it."

· 12 ·

The Baritone Plan in the Cathedral Diocesan Choir of Brooklyn

Monsignor Lawrence H. Bracken, founder of the Cathedral Diocesan Choir of Brooklyn and its conductor for twenty-one years up to 1944, worked out a plan for keeping his choirboys in the choir during the period when their voices were changing. Since he did not give the plan a name, I have called it the "baritone" plan to distinguish it from the other plans described in this study.

In the "baritone" plan, the older boy soprano is transferred to alto when signs of adolescence are observed in his speaking voice or his physique. When the changed voice first develops, he is classified as "baritone" and he sings what he can of the bass part, being warned not to reach for high or low notes. He understands he is not a baritone in the usual sense of the word, and no attempt is made to predict whether the voice will become tenor or bass. The boy is told that his voice will continue to lower, that the range will extend up and down as his voice develops, and that the voice will gradually take on a definite timbre as it matures to tenor or bass. Every boy's voice passes through the "baritone" stage, although occasionally a boy will go directly from alto to tenor (as in Case E below).

EVOLUTION OF THE BARITONE PLAN

Explaining how he came to evolve his plan, Monsignor Bracken said: "No adolescent boy ever had to leave the choir on account of his changing voice. From the start of my work with the choir, I have had the boy singing during the changing period. My principal reasons at first for doing this were: I found that the boys were able to sing the alto part, and they did not want to leave the choir any more than I wanted to see them go. I have never found a group of professional male altos satisfactory, for the tone quality of the individual voices varies so much in character that it is impossible to get a homogeneous tone from them as a group.

This fact induced me to try and make an alto section from my own boys. Although I never accepted the tradition that a boy should rest his voice during adolescence, I did have, during my early experience with the choir, several cases where boys had to stop singing for a period. With my present plan, which is the result of years of observation of my boys, I have never had any case of loss of voice."

The choir quota aimed for at the start of a new season was forty sopranos, twenty altos, sixteen tenors, and twenty-four basses. (The choir gallery has an unusually large seating accommodation—for over one hundred.) One season all members of the men's sections, except two, a tenor and a bass, both professional singers, were individuals who had sung in the choir since they were sopranos. The oldest bass was twenty-five, and he had been in the choir fifteen years. The other basses were between fourteen and twenty-two. The five oldest tenors were between twenty-two and twenty-seven. Three of them had been in the choir for fifteen years; the other tenors were between fifteen and twenty. The two professionals did the solo work and helped to make the tone of the men's sections sound more mature.

The evolution of the baritone plan was aided by the fact that it was possible to start a season with a larger number of sopranos than the quota. To keep up a supply of "new" boys for the soprano section, each year after Easter an announcement calling for boys between the ages of nine and eleven was sent to all the parochial schools in Brooklyn. All who responded were accepted as "new" boys, and no individual tests were given. These boys met once a week by themselves, and twice a week with the regular choir boys until the summer vacation began. The rehearsals for the new boys only, were devoted to voice training and instruction in reading music. At the other rehearsals the new boys began to learn their business by actual participation in the regular work of the choir.

After a few rehearsals, individual tests were given to the new boys, but as part of the rehearsal procedure and not specifically for examination purposes. The boy won a place in the choir from the interest he displayed through regular attendance at rehearsals. After the summer vacation he might become a member of the choir.

The schedule of rehearsals for the choir was as follows:

Sopranos	Three 80-minute sessions a week
Altos	Two 80-minute sessions a week
Tenors	One two-hour session a week
Basses	One two-hour session a week
Altos, Tenors, and Basses	One two-hour session a week
Full Choir	One hour session a week

In addition to the above schedule, those tenors and basses who were old enough to have left school and whose voices were above average were given individual lessons in small groups as regularly as the week's program permitted.

The choir's program provided for one High Mass a week and special musical services in other churches in and out of the diocese. Like the liturgical part of the services, most of the choral work was *a cappella,* all combinations of voices up to S.S.A.A.T.T.B.B. being used. Occasionally the sopranos were divided into three parts. Choruses from the masses and oratorios were used with accompaniment at the special musical services.

The choir supported itself by giving an annual concert at the Brooklyn Academy of Music Opera House. Only the two professionals were paid for their services in the choir. The rest were invited to spend two to three weeks at the choir's summer camp every year. This way of recognizing their services proved to have a strong influence in building up a choir spirit. A system of fines for absence from rehearsals without proper excuse, and for other irregularities, determined the length of a boy's stay at camp. The new boys were also invited to camp, but for a shorter period, their record of attendance at rehearsals being taken into consideration. Music was a part of the camp program; the new boys, for instance, had three short rehearsals daily to prepare them to take their places in the choir at the beginning of the season.

CLASSIFICATION IN THE BARITONE PLAN

By Monsignor Bracken's plan, members of the choir are tested three times a year: after Easter, after the summer vacation, and after Christmas. Between tests a boy's classification is not changed unless it is really necessary for the sake of his future voice; for example, if an alto's voice suddenly changes, he is transferred to baritone before the time for the next test.

In the soprano section the objective is a light floating tone rather than bigness. The importance of breath control and listening is emphasized from the day the boy enters the choir; thus, from the start he is trained to form good habits as a chorister.

Soprano to Alto. A soprano is transferred to alto when signs of adolescence begin to be noticeable in his speaking voice and his physique. As he has had some experience in singing a second part (as Soprano II), he is a useful alto from the start, but effectiveness in the lower range is not looked for until he has been in the alto section for some time.

Because the membership of the alto section always changes to some extent after a test, the problem is to maintain a satisfactory section for an entire season. To meet this problem, as many sopranos as possible are transferred to the alto section at the beginning of a season, so that there will be a sufficient number to make up for the loss of altos during the year. This weakens the soprano section, but a group of new boys is ready for the choir every September.

Alto to Baritone. As soon as the boy looks like a young man and his voice has lowered so that he can produce a good E (bass), he is transferred to baritone, no matter how much of the alto range remains.

Baritone to Tenor. The boy whose voice is developing to tenor is transferred as soon as a tenor timbre is noted and there is a fair degree of control over the changed voice at high E (bass). As a baritone, he is likely to have used the falsetto in this region, but the changed voice has been maturing and the range developing upward. Because of the three tests given during the year, it is not possible for a boy to remain a baritone longer than he should—once it is evident that the voice will become tenor and not bass.

Alto to Tenor. On the basis of his physique and his age, an alto who retains his unchanged voice for a longer time than usual is transferred to tenor if a few notes below low G (treble clef) have developed. This change is desirable for psychological reasons, for the boy should now be treated as an adult chorister; and although he is not ready to sing tenor in the lower range, lower notes have a chance to develop if he is in the tenor section.

The "Compromise" Alto. A compromise is made with the baritone plan when a boy in the alto section can sing in either the changed or the unchanged voice without difficulty and has an alto range of over an octave. Outside of the choir, at school assemblies or in informal singing, the boy usually sings in his changed voice. To the choir he is more useful as an alto than as a baritone. If he continues to keep an alto range of over an octave while his changed voice is developing, and if he is a good alto, he is selected to be what may be termed a "compromise" alto when the alto section is weak. There can be no objection to this if he is not kept singing alto too long to the detriment of the development of his future voice.

One year, for example, during the period from October to February, it was foreseen that after the Easter test held in early April there would be too few altos for the beginning of the next season, September, to make an effective section if the regular plan of dealing with the altos was carried out. Consequently, some who would have been transferred to baritone after the summer vacation were kept in the alto section up to Christmas. Their changed voices had begun to develop before the summer vacation, but because these boys were still able to sing comfortably in the alto range, they were used as "compromise" altos. The factors that determined the length of time a boy should remain a "compromise" alto were his physique and his speaking voice. When he looked like a young man and had the speaking voice of a young man, he was transferred to baritone. Thus, while the compromise was made for the sake of the choir work, it was never at the expense of the boy's voice.

THE BARITONE PLAN VERSUS THE ALTO-TENOR PLAN

When I had an opportunity to observe the baritone plan in operation, the question that constantly occurred to me was: Is the alto-tenor plan not a better one? It should be remembered that the boy in the Cathedral Diocesan Choir of Brooklyn knows why he is classified as baritone, and he knows how to use his voice while so classified. He also knows that his voice will change later to tenor or bass.

In the baritone plan, by singing what he can of the bass part, a boy whose voice is going to be tenor has the opportunity to use his lower range, but he does not get any opportunity to use the upper part of his range. When it becomes evident that the voice is developing into tenor and the boy is transferred to the tenor section, he is likely to have some difficulty with the highest notes because he has not used his upper range. In the alto-tenor plan the boy whose voice is developing into tenor does not have this difficulty, for the lower part of the alto-tenor range becomes the upper part of the tenor range as the voice gradually matures towards the changed status, and the highest notes are easier to control because the voice has never been out of action. Therefore, one may say that the alto-tenor plan is better for the voice which becomes tenor, while for the voice which becomes bass the baritone plan is suitable.

The alto-tenor plan has been successful mainly because a special corpus of school music has been composed and arranged for it. Since liturgical music of the polyphonic type to suit the alto-tenor plan is not likely to be written, the alto-tenor plan is no more successful with a church choir than it was for schools before the specially arranged music was available. But a great amount of the old polyphonic sacred music does suit boys' changing voices. This is the kind that forms the greater part of the repertoire of the Cathedral Diocesan Choir of Brooklyn. For this reason the baritone plan is good for this choir. It seemed to me that one of the striking features of the choir's singing was the tone of the tenor section; it had a real tenor timbre, not mature, but fresh and unforced, and it was very effective and easily heard in the ensemble.

VOICE HISTORIES FROM THE BARITONE PLAN

From the point of view of retaining the musical interests of boys during the change-of-voice period, it may be useful to set down some practical evidence about the changing voices in the Cathedral Diocesan Choir of

Brooklyn. Following are: (*1*) voice histories of a group of older boy altos through the period of mutation up to a time when the changed voices had developed to a considerable extent; (*2*) data about a group of boys who became tenor after being classified for a period as baritones; (*3*) data about the voice histories of baritones who had been "compromise" altos; and (*4*) voice histories of some future tenors whose voices during the changing period did not suit the baritone plan of classification.

The Future of the Boy Alto. One year just before the summer vacation, in the alto section there were seven older boy altos on whom the effectiveness of the section had depended: Cases A to G. All except Case F were ready to be transferred to baritone after the vacation, and all except Cases D and E had been singing alto for two months. Case D had been in the alto section for fifteen months, and Case E for an entire season. After the summer vacation Cases A and B were classified as baritones, Case A being transferred to tenor nine months later, finally becoming a very satisfactory tenor, and Case B remaining baritone up to the end of the season. Cases C, D, and G were used as compromise altos up to Christmas, at which time they were transferred to the baritone section where they remained to the end of the season. Case E remained alto for two months after the vacation, and was then transferred to tenor, skipping the baritone classification, and he turned out to be a first rate tenor. Case F remained alto for the entire season after the vacation, during which period his voice seemed to be changing to tenor, but it suddenly developed to a deep bass after he had sung tenor for three months.

CASE A

Just before the summer vacation, this boy's weight was 120 pounds and his age fourteen. He had been in the alto section two months. The range of his unchanged voice was $F_{|}$ sharp to A', that is, over two octaves, and his changed voice had developed down to $b_{|}$ flat. He passed from the unchanged to the changed voice without any break.

During the summer vacation, the upper notes of his unchanged voice disappeared, and after the vacation the range of the changed voice was $g_{|}$ to g' (that is, two octaves), the timbre being more like tenor than baritone. The speaking voice had changed; he was classified as baritone. At the September test, when he sang a descending scale, his unchanged voice broke at $B_{|}$ flat in passing to the changed voice, but at later tests there was no break.

By Christmas, the range of his changed voice had not altered except that f' was his upper limit. He passed into the falsetto at this note and sang to A. He was still in the baritone classification, but the upper notes were taking on a tenor timbre. Two months after Christmas he had difficulty with the upper notes of his changed voice. He passed into the falsetto at E flat. The lack of control in the upper range kept him in the baritone classification, although it seemed that the voice might become tenor.

After being baritone for about nine months, he was transferred to tenor after the Easter test. His range was $g_{|}$ to g' (that is, two octaves), and he had gained considerable control of his upper notes. He still passed easily into the falsetto. From Christmas to the end of the season he never sang lower than $g_{|}$, this being evidence that his voice had dropped to its limit.

Three years after the first test, the boy's weight was 136 pounds (an increase of sixteen pounds), and he had grown one inch taller. He had developed into quite a mature tenor for his age (seventeen years). His range was two octaves from $g_{|}$, and he could sing falsetto to D'.

CASE B

Just before the summer vacation, this boy's weight was 124 pounds and his age fifteen. He had been in the alto section two months. The range of his unchanged voice was $G_{|}$ to G', and his changed voice, $g_{|}$ to b flat. He had difficulty above b flat.

After the vacation, he was classified as baritone, his changed voice range being $g_{|}$ to g', and his unchanged voice range $B_{|}$ flat to G'. The unchanged voice faded away at the $B_{|}$ flat, and there was a gap in the scale (to $G_{|}$) from this note. It disappeared after he began to sing regularly again. No doubt the gap resulted because the boy had not been singing during the summer vacation while the changed voice was developing rapidly. During the vacation, his weight had increased twelve pounds, an indication that the physiological growth had been considerable.

Three weeks before Christmas, the speaking voice was noted as "mannish"; his range was $g_{|}$ to e' flat. He was able to pass into the falsetto at F. He had gained another two pounds in weight. He remained in the baritone classification until the end of the season, at which time his weight was 149 pounds (an increase of twenty-five pounds during the season) and the range of his changed voice had extended down one note (to $f_{|}$). He broke passing into the falsetto. At the February test, he had passed into the falsetto at D, and the falsetto range was D to G. When the boys who were present at this test were asked what they thought his classification should be, the majority said "tenor," while most of the others were in doubt. The tone quality was light baritone, bright in character. Although this boy remained in the baritone classification until the end of the season, the only prediction that could be made was that the voice might become tenor or high baritone when it settled.

CASE C

Just before the summer vacation, this boy's weight was 124 pounds, his height 5′ 5″, and his age thirteen. He had been in the alto section two months. The range of his unchanged voice was $A_{|}$ to E', and he could sing down to e in an alto-tenor quality.

After the vacation, the unchanged voice range was G_1 to F', and the changed voice range, b_1 to e'; but because he had difficulty finding his changed voice, he was kept in the alto section.

Three weeks before Christmas, he had lost the highest notes of his alto range, and he could sing in what was left of the unchanged voice down to A_1 flat. His speaking voice was adolescent; he still had difficulty in finding his changed voice, and its range had not altered. He was now 5′ 6″ tall.

Two months after Christmas, his speaking voice had changed, and it had an adolescent tinge. His boy's voice had disappeared. He was transferred to baritone, his range being g_1 to e' flat. By the end of the season, there was no change in the range, but some tonal development was noted.

By November, his weight was 150 pounds (an increase of twenty-six pounds in seventeen months). He could sing in his falsetto voice the scale of B flat (soprano) down to A_1. The range of his changed voice remained the same. He was now an acceptable baritone.

A boy of rather large proportions, plump though not very heavy, he was shy at every test. I felt he never quite did himself justice. The choirmaster thought he was inclined to be slow mentally. I was never able to diagnose his difficulties, but they may have been due, in part, to his shyness. Although he took his tests earnestly, he did not seem to be able to get control of his voice. He was as a rule languid. A year after the last test, he left the choir of his own accord.

CASE D

Just before the summer vacation, this boy's weight was 116 pounds, his age fifteen. He had been alto for fifteen months. The range of his unchanged voice was G_1 to G', and his changed voice g_1 to b flat. At b flat he passed easily into the unchanged voice. After the vacation, he had difficulty singing alto at the start of the season; the range of his unchanged voice was G_1 to B, and he could sing from g_1 to e' in his changed voice. He was used as a "compromise" alto.

Three weeks before Christmas, his changed voice range was a_1 to d', and he could sing falsetto to B flat. His speaking voice had changed and was pleasant in quality. He was 5′ 4″ tall.

A month after Christmas, he was transferred to baritone, his range being g_1 to d', and he still could pass easily into the falsetto. He remained in the baritone classification until the end of the season.

His range had not altered by November of the next season, and the tone had not developed as much as one would have expected. He could still sing falsetto to B flat. He now weighed 125 pounds and his height was 5′ 5″.

This boy was a very satisfactory "compromise" alto. His difficulty in singing alto after the summer vacation was probably due to the fact that he had not been using his unchanged voice for a time, and it would have been more natural for him to sing in his changed voice which had developed to a range of over an octave. At later tests, he had no difficulty. The voice seemed to be developing into a good baritone, though the tonal development at the last test was less than expected.

CASE E

This boy had been a good soprano soloist. He sang alto for an entire season. Just before the summer vacation, when he was sixteen, he weighed 150 pounds. His range was B_1 to B'. He could also sing down to b_1 flat. The first signs of his changed voice had been observed a few weeks previously.

After the summer vacation, he remained in the alto section. His range was G_1 to A'. The lowest note of his changed voice was still b_1 flat, and he passed easily into the falsetto. A month before Christmas, he was transferred to tenor because of his physique and his speaking voice, which had changed. However, enough of the boy voice remained to have kept him as an alto. He had gained twenty pounds in six months. He was at this time six feet tall. Six weeks after Christmas, the tenor quality was darkish, and he had gained an inch in height.

By November of the next season, his changed voice range was b_1 flat to f' sharp, and the tone quality was that of a fairly mature tenor. He could sing falsetto to F'. Two years later, his range was b_1 to g', and he seemed to have stopped growing. He had increased in weight to 175 pounds.

As an alto, at fifteen, he was tall and his physique above average. From his physique and the length of time he had been singing alto, one would have expected to note the changed voice developing before it did. An explanation of the sudden development of the change might be that it had been happening unknown to the boy. Being a fine alto, he had no urge to find his changed voice (in the choir); several times I asked him to try to sing in the changed voice. Note that the changed voice had lowered to its limit (b_1 flat) at the time of the first test, and that he gained twenty pounds during the six months following, at the end of which period his height was six feet—evidence of his physiological growth and that he could have been classified as tenor after the vacation.

CASE F

This boy started to sing alto after the Easter test, and he remained in the alto section for fifteen months, that is, up to the end of the next season. Just before the summer vacation, his weight was 124 pounds and his age thirteen. The range of his unchanged voice was B_1 to A'.

After the summer vacation, his speaking voice was adolescent and his range d to G'. The quality of the lowest notes gave no indication that the changed voice was developing. Six weeks later, he had lost a few of his highest notes; his range was e to E'. He was 5′ 11½″ tall. Three months later, his weight was 140 pounds; his speaking voice had developed to the youth stage. His range was d to F', and he was six feet tall. By the end of the season he could sing down to b_1 flat. His voice had taken on a slight tenor timbre: he was now 6′ 1″ tall and still in the alto section.

He was transferred to tenor after having been alto for fifteen months. His range was b_{I} to f', and he could reach A' in his falsetto. After singing tenor for three months, he was transferred to bass, for his voice had lowered to a bass range, and his speaking voice indicated that it was going to be bass. Four months later his height was 6′ 3″ and his voice baritone in timbre, the range being f_{I} to e'. By the end of the season (seven months later), his range was e_{I} flat to e' flat, and he could sing falsetto to D'; but he found it difficult to find his falsetto. His voice broke at G singing a descending scale.

The voice history of this boy calls for some observations. He was tall and always lanky while he was an alto. He grew rapidly in height without putting on much weight. During the summer vacation, the voice lowered about a fifth, but the highest notes did not disappear, as is the usual pattern; he could sing up to G'. Lack of any sign of the changed voice developing in the lower range also was contrary to the usual patern. During the season, the highest notes he had been able to sing easily began to be difficult, and during the second half of the season, he lost his upper range. Only two low notes in the bass clef, c and b_{I} flat, developed during the entire season. Just before the second summer vacation, the changed voice began to emerge, and after the vacation he was transferred to tenor. There was still quite a part of the unchanged voice left.

From the boy's history up to this point, one would have expected that the voice would develop into tenor because of the slow rate at which it had been lowering and developing to the changed status. The usual pattern, however, did not follow. The highest notes did not disappear as new low notes developed. The boy was only three months in the tenor section, for he had difficulty at e' to f'. Once he was in the bass section, the voice developed and matured at a very rapid rate, and his general growth was beyond the normal. When he was transferred to tenor, his weight was 149 pounds, his height 6′ 1″, and his age fifteen. A year later, his weight had increased thirty-one pounds, and his height was 6′ 3″. During the next eight months after this, his growth slowed down; he weighed 186 pounds, and his height was 6′ 3¾″.

With this boy there was never any problem of attitude towards his voice, as there sometimes is with a boy whose growth rate is so rapid. He was content to let nature take its course. He did not mind singing alto even though he was six feet tall; nor did he worry that his man's voice was slow in developing; but once it was evident that he was going to have a fine bass voice, he began to glory in it. Rather shy as an alto, as a young bass he got over this and began to take any opportunity that presented itself to sing songs that would show off his low bass notes. Incidentally, he was a fine baseball player; the Brooklyn Dodgers were keeping an eye on him. I did not know about this until the last test, when, after a remark about his physique in relation to his voice, the other boys told me about his prowess in baseball.

CASE G

Just before the summer vacation, this boy's weight was 120 pounds, and his age fourteen. He had been in the alto section for two months. His range was

G_{I} to G^{I}. His changed voice had developed down to b_{I} flat. After the vacation, the range of his unchanged voice was G_{I} to F^{I}, and his changed voice had not lowered any further. The voice had therefore developed very little during the vacation. His weight, however, had increased seventeen pounds. His speaking voice had changed, and he could pass easily from the changed to the unchanged voice. The voice seemed to be changing quickly now. He was used as a "compromise" alto up to Christmas. A month after Christmas, he was transferred to bass, and two months later, the range was g_{I} to e^{I} flat. His speaking voice now was deep and somewhat husky.

It was thought that this boy had been used as a "compromise" alto too long, for towards Christmas the boy voice began to disappear so quickly that he found singing the alto part difficult.

Alto to Tenor via Baritone. One season just before the summer vacation, there were twelve boys classified as baritones. After the vacation, four (Cases H, J, K, and L) were transferred to the tenor section, and, after three years in it, the voices gave every indication that they would remain tenor. All four could be labeled "slowly changing," for it took Case H thirty months, Cases J and K each seventeen months, and Case L forty-one months, to become tenor from the time they were first classified as alto. The chart shows the progress of the voices from the time they entered the alto section, the period they were in the baritone classification before being transferred to tenor, and their progress as tenors during a period of fourteen months.

"Compromise" Alto to Baritone. Data about four baritones who had been "compromise" altos are given in the chart below.

Cases M and N were altos for an entire season, part of the time as "compromise" altos. They were transferred to the baritone classification after the summer vacation, and finally became basses. After eight months as baritones, M's development during the six months following was that of a young bass who gradually loses what is left of the unchanged voice; N's followed the same pattern, except that at the end of six months all signs of the boy voice seemed to have gone. M became a baritone (in the usual sense of the word) and N a bass. N's difficulty, after being baritone for eight months, may have been due to the lack of control over that part of the alto range which develops into the upper baritone range, for the voice was developing to bass rather than baritone. After the summer vacation, the difficulty disappeared, and he was able to sing to A in the falsetto.

Case O remained in the alto section for a much longer period than usual, part of the time as a "compromise" alto. Accordingly, the voice might have been considered a slowly changing one likely to become tenor. During the first three months the boy was classified as baritone, it was a

Data about Four Boys Who Became Tenor after Being Classified for a Period as "Baritones"

	Case H	Case J	Case K	Case L
Age when transferred to Alto	13 years and 7 months	14 years	13 years and 5 months	13 years and 5 months
Period in Alto section	18 months	12 months	10 months	24 months
Period in Baritone classification	12 months	5 months	7 months	17 months
Range after being in Tenor section for three months	$a_{\mid}$ to $f^{\mid}$: and then he passed into the boy's voice	$b_{\mid}$ to $f^{\mid}$: tone light in quality	$b_{\mid}\flat$ to $f^{\mid}$: $f^{\mid}$ difficult	$a_{\mid}$ to $f^{\mid}$: and then he passed into the boy's voice to $B\flat$; timbre, tenor
Range two months later	$a_{\mid}$ to $e^{\mid}$: tone bright and open	$b_{\mid}\flat$ to $f^{\mid}$: tone had developed a little	No change in range: $f^{\mid}$ easier; tone darkish in color	$b_{\mid}\flat$ to $d^{\mid}$: difficulty above $d^{\mid}$, which may have been due to a cold
Range nine months later than previous date (summer vacation included in this period)	$g_{\mid}$ to $e^{\mid}$: he broke in passing to the falsetto at $d^{\mid}$; voice unsettled and timbre difficult to determine	$b_{\mid}$ to $f^{\mid}\sharp$: tonally less mature than expected	$a_{\mid}$ to $e^{\mid}$: tonal development reasonably good	$a_{\mid}$ to $D^{\mid}$: a little difficulty with $f^{\mid}$; singing an ascending scale, he passed easily into the falsetto below $f^{\mid}$

question whether his voice was developing to tenor or bass. The timbre was adolescent tenor, possibly because he had been singing alto so long.

Case P had been in the habit of experimenting with his voice after the change took place—but outside of the choir. Because he had been a useful alto, he was put back from baritone into the alto section, which was weak at the time, and he remained in it for almost nine months before he was shifted back to baritone. (The summer vacation was part of the nine months.) The timbre of the changed voice had always seemed to indicate it would be bass, but the boy's history shows he kept his boy voice for a longer time than usual for the type of bass he became.

The boy had been a good soprano, and he enjoyed finding out what he could do with his changed voice while he was in the alto section. A year after the last test shown in the chart, his weight was 155 pounds, his height 5′ 11″, and his range e$_{|}$ to d' flat. He had difficulty above d'. He could sing falsetto to D' flat, but he could not pass from the changed to the unchanged voice without a break. The voice was mature bass for the boy's age, but it was still unsettled. It was thought his difficulies arose because he experimented with his voice too much during the mutation period. He was impatient, too, at the slow development of his upper notes, which he wanted to use in songs for the bass voice. Two years after the last test, he was able to sing f', but only on a full voice. He still kept experimenting with the high notes over which he had not gained complete control.

Tenors Who Did Not Suit the Baritone Plan. During the course of four years of observation of the boys' voices in the Cathedral Diocesan Choir of Brooklyn, it was noted that only three altos became tenors without going through the baritone classification. One was Case E, whose history has already been given. The voice histories of the other two (Cases Q and R) follow. Both were in the baritone classification, but for a very short period because this classification did not suit their voice development.

CASE Q

This boy, age fourteen, was large and fat, with a short neck—the type physically that often becomes tenor. From his physical appearance he would have been taken to be much older. After singing alto for seven months, he began to find notes around G sharp difficult, and below B$_{|}$ a slight tinge of the changed voice could be detected. Two months later G sharp and notes above this had almost disappeared, and the lower part of the voice had taken on the timbre of a young tenor. He was transferred to baritone. After singing in this classification for five weeks, he reported that he felt uncomfortable, so he was transferred to the tenor section, though it was only a few weeks to the next test. His range was checked, and he was told to sing strictly within it for some time.

Voice Histories of Baritones Who Had Been "Compromise" Altos

	Case M	Case N	Case O	Case P
Age when transferred to Alto	14 years and 4 months	14 years and 9 months	Almost 17	14 years and 9 months
In Alto section	An entire season	An entire season	Three years and 3 months	Two years, during which period he was a "compromise" Alto for 9 months. (The summer vacation is included in the 9 months.)
Transferred to Baritone	After the summer vacation	After the summer vacation	After the Christmas test	After the Christmas test. After Easter he was put back to the Alto section to be a "compromise" Alto, being transferred to Baritone 4 months after the summer vacation.
After 8 months in the Baritone classification	There was an adolescent tinge in the upper range, and this part of the voice might have been called alto-tenor. Weight: 116 pounds	Difficulty with notes above $b\flat$. Weight: 130 pounds	After 3 months it was difficult to say whether the voice was going to be tenor or bass. He remained Baritone to the end of the season. Weight: 170 pounds	His range at the end of 6 months as a Baritone was $f_{\mid}$ to $b\flat$; and then he broke passing into the falsetto. Weight: 141 pounds
Range at start of next season	$g_{\mid}$ to $e^{\mid}$: and then he passed into the falsetto for a few notes. Weight: 132 pounds	$g_{\mid}$ to $d^{\mid}$: and then he passed into the falsetto up to A. Weight: 135 pounds	$g_{\mid}$ to $e^{\mid}$: a promising Baritone whose voice had developed considerably. Weight: 175 pounds	His lowest note was $e_{\mid}\flat$. He broke passing into the boy voice at $b\flat$ at one test, and at $d^{\mid}$ at another.
Range 3 months later	$g_{\mid}$ to $d^{\mid}$: and some of the boy voice still remained. A young bass, but the tone had not developed as much as was expected. Weight: 134 pounds	$g_{\mid}$ to $e^{\mid}\flat$: tone, big. A great deal of development noted. All signs of the boy voice seemed to have gone. Weight: 136 pounds	$f_{\mid}$ to $f^{\mid}$: a serviceable Baritone; tone quality mellow and dark in color. Weight: 175 pounds	$f_{\mid}$ to $d^{\mid}$. The voice broke passing into the falsetto at one attempt of a test, and the quality of the falsetto was good in spite of the fact that he had not been using his falsetto for a year. Weight: 145 pounds

After a month in the tenor section, his changed voice developed to the extent that he had a good e flat, and the tone quality was decidedly tenor. He found f' difficult.

Just before the summer vacation, his range was d to f', f' still being difficult. He was beginning to be of some value as a tenor. After the vacation, his range was $b_{|}$ flat to f', and he could pass into the falsetto to A. At this time he weighed 170 pounds. By Christmas, he had become a serviceable tenor; his weight was now 180 pounds.

It should be noted that the rate at which this voice changed to tenor was more rapid than usual—approximately one year from the time that it was first classified as alto. It would have been unwise to have kept this boy singing alto any longer than he did. The five weeks in the baritone classification gave his changed voice a chance to develop.

CASE R

This boy had been alto for one year and baritone for one month. Just before the summer vacation, he had been in the tenor section for three weeks. His range was e flat to g'. He was fifteen years of age and weighed 129 pounds. After the vacation, his range was e to B flat, and he remained in the tenor section. A month before Christmas, his range was c to g'. He had a few notes higher than g' in his falsetto voice, but of a very indifferent character. His speaking voice was that of a youth. By Christmas, his weight had increased sixteen pounds in six months, and his range was $b_{|}$ flat to d', d' being difficult. The timbre was developing to tenor.

From Christmas to the end of the season, the boy had a falsetto range of a few notes only. Sometimes there was a break passing into or from the falsetto, but not always at the same note. His range at the end of the season was $b_{|}$ to g'.

During the summer following, I used the boy at a demonstration lecture before a summer school class and made the following report about him: "The voice is still very uncertain. He can do unexpectedly something different every time he sings. The voice was interesting for demonstration purposes. He is beginning to fill out and physically he now looks like a young man except that his face is rather boyish looking."

By November (of the second season), his range was $a_{|}$ to B flat, and his weight 140 pounds (a loss of four pounds from Christmas). He was now sixteen years of age. While he could easily pass to and from the falsetto, occasionally there was a break. He remained in the tenor classification.

· 13 ·

The Counter-Tenor Plan of St. Luke's Choristers, California

A plan of dealing with the adolescent boy's voice known as the counter-tenor plan is used by William Ripley Dorr at St. Luke's Church, Long Beach, California. His choir, known as the St. Luke's Choristers, is trained according to the method used by Father Finn with his Paulist Choristers in Chicago.[1] For several years Mr. Dorr and his boys have been making motion picture sound recordings, and they have appeared in several film productions, including *Mrs. Miniver, Random Harvest,* and *The Corn is Green.* The choir, consisting of some sixty men and boys, is divided into Soprano I and II, Counter-Tenor I and II, Tenor I and II, Baritone, and Bass. The sopranos number around twenty and the counter-tenors (older boys who sing the alto part), fifteen.

Mr. Dorr developed an interest in the method after observing the training of the choirboys in England and noting the problems that the choirmasters had with the alto sections. "Where adult male altos were not used," he said, "the altos were boys who sang with a chest tone when they should really have been singing soprano; or they were worn-out sopranos whose voices were changing, but who sang as altos until they had to be dropped from the choir." Mr. Dorr did not like the tone of male adult altos. Hearing about the Paulist Choristers, he became a pupil of Father Finn, and was convinced that the plan of training the adolescent boy as a counter-tenor to sing the alto part solved the alto problem for male choirs in America.

Speaking of the plan, Mr. Dorr remarked: Father Finn "develops a boy-soprano tone, which is built up in range and power from a *pianissimo* hum in the head voice. It is a floating, ethereal quality of tone of great beauty that is ideal for sacred music. Father Finn found that a boy who had mastered this training is in nearly every case able to be trained as a

[1] The method is described in William J. Finn, *The Art of the Choral Conductor* (Boston, Birchard, 1939), Chapter VIII.

counter-tenor, for he can keep control over the lower part of his erstwhile boy voice during the entire adolescent period and sing a lovely alto, of the same general character of the soprano tone, but darker and fuller. This system of training boy sopranos ensures a supply of voices for the alto section. By means of it my sopranos and counter-tenors are able to sing four-part music for boys' voices with a good tone and balance."

CLASSIFICATION AND TRAINING IN THE COUNTER-TENOR PLAN

The term "counter-tenor" dates back to the sixteenth century. It was used for the male voice of the highest pitch, the adult male alto. *Grove's Dictionary* gives the compass of the voice as "limited to notes admissible on the staff which had the C clef on its third line; that is, to notes a sixth above and below middle C. Later this compass was extended by bringing into use the third register of the voice, the falsetto, a register often strongest with those whose voices are naturally bass." This latter type of voice is the adult male alto that is found in church choirs in England and in some Episcopal church choirs in America.

Explaining his use of "counter-tenor" for "alto" as a classification, Mr. Dorr said: "After the second soprano stage all boys who are adolescent are called counter-tenors, the adolescent boy being one whose speaking voice has begun to change from the boyish treble. A boy alto is a pre-adolescent boy who has a real alto voice, and such voices are exceedingly rare. I have not had a dozen in thirty years. One that I had, was a first soprano who developed beautiful notes from middle C down to alto G. I used him as alto soloist, and he sang with the counter-tenors; but as his speaking voice showed no signs of change, I called him alto. The part that the counter-tenors sing is the alto part. In rehearsal I speak of the alto part, but the singers I call counter-tenors."

At first Mr. Dorr transferred a boy from soprano to counter-tenor either when his speaking voice showed unmistakable evidence of the change or when he had the slightest difficulty in singing his part. Now he transfers him when he is able to sing a good firm tone on tenor C (octave below middle C). This means that the changed voice has developed down to this note. At the time I was consulting Mr. Dorr about his work, the second soprano section consisted of twelve boys, only two of whom had unchanged speaking voices.

The counter-tenors range in age from fourteen to eighteen. Because there are usually so many, they are transferred to the men's section at their own request when they are sixteen or seventeen, even though they could sing counter-tenor for some time longer. However, after having had a taste of making recordings for the films, the boys exhibited an interesting change of attitude towards singing counter-tenor. Commenting on this, Mr. Dorr said: "The psychological factor is apparently an important one—possibly fully as important as the physiological one. Formerly a boy wished to be transferred to the men's section, not because he had any objection to singing counter-tenor, but because he wanted to have the prestige of being in the men's section with only one rehearsal a week. Now, because of the movie work, he wants to stay as long as possible in the boys' section because he enjoys movie work and finds it lucrative." Boys remain counter-tenors for varying lengths of time, sometimes from two to three years, "and it does not as yet make any difference what the voice will finally become."

It may be noted that the St. Luke's Choir has made an album of *Familiar Hymns* (Capitol Records). In the hymn, "Now the Day Is Over," there is a fine example of a counter-tenor singing one verse as a solo accompanied by the choir.

The method of training the counter-tenors is to use downward vocalization exercises, never starting any higher than E' (soprano clef), bringing the voice down over the break to B, flat (second line, bass clef). I remarked that he might be able to do this with the counter-tenors as a group, but that surely few of them were able to sing this range individually. Mr. Dorr's answer was that all but the very youngest counter-tenors sing this range and many of them have a wider range. "Singing over the break," he explained thus: "The boy picks up the idea from the others, and usually all that is necessary is to tell him to sing with a yawning sensation and a very relaxed jaw."

Asked what criteria he had set up for transferring a counter-tenor to tenor or bass, Mr. Dorr replied: "I pay no attention to the boy's counter-tenor voice. If he can sing the bass parts in our music and wants to change, I transfer him if there is room for him in the bass section. The same holds good for tenors. However, it more often happens that I have to transfer a boy from the counter-tenor section to make room for boys who are obliged to move out of the soprano section. The important point is that most counter-tenors can continue to sing counter-tenor until they are about twenty, at which age their voices begin to harden and become like the adult male alto, which voice does not blend well with the others. So unless I lose boys who go to college, I have to move them to the men's section to make room for new counter-tenors." By way of illustration he referred to the following cases:

A) A counter-tenor whose voice was developing into a promising baritone: at the age of seventeen, when he weighed 150 pounds and his height was 6′ 2″, he had to leave the choir for a season. After being away for a year he came back for the summer. He then had a fine baritone voice, but he could still sing counter-tenor; so he sang whichever part was needed most during the vacation.

B) A boy sixteen years of age, height 5′ 8″, and weight 140 pounds, a second bass who had a very good low C: he was able to sing the alto part in "Lift Thine Eyes" most effectively, and he was used as a counter-tenor in recording work.

C) A fine tenor, 20 years of age, who often sang counter-tenor in S.S.A.A. numbers just because he enjoyed doing so.

THE ADULT COUNTER-TENOR

G. Edward Stubbs in his book *The Adult Male Alto or Counter-Tenor Voice* (New York, H. W. Gray, 1908) distinguishes between two varieties of the adult counter-tenor voice: (*1*) the high, light tenor whose range is $A_{\prime}$ to $D^{\prime}$. This voice has the following characteristics: the chest and falsetto tones are readily joined, and they are so often blended by nature that it is impossible to detect a difference of register in any part of the vocal range; the upper tones are easily reached, are entirely free from strain, and are full and rich; the lower tones, although less powerful and sonorous than in the ordinary tenor, are remarkably pure and free from coarseness. A distinguishing mark of this voice is that the conversational and the singing tones correspond, the former being pitched near the middle of the range. (*2*) The falsetto alto in which the falsetto register is distinctly different from the chest register; in which there is a break that can be eradicated only by careful training in early adult life; and in which the colloquial and the singing tones do not correspond.

Stubbs says the first voice is the better of the two, but even when round and resonant and possessing all the attributes generally looked for in the well-cultivated voice, it is often criticized as being unnatural, especially if the range is of unusual extent. He says that hundreds of men's voices never undergo mutation, and women's voices of tenor and baritone range are not as rare as they are supposed to be.[2] The owners of male voices that never change "misunderstand their own singing powers; they do not seek vocal training, but yield quietly to the tyranny of musical fashion, and endeavor to hide what they consider a vocal defect."

THE COUNTER-TENOR PLAN AND THE SCHOOLS

The counter-tenor plan, as it has evolved to solve the problem of the adolescent boy who sings the alto part in male choirs, could be used in schools. Mr. Dorr uses it in the schools of Palos Verdes, California, and

[2] On the *Magic Key Program,* June 12, 1938, Madame Ann de Ohla broadcast over NBC, singing as a soprano, as a contralto, as a tenor, and as a bass.

he says he has been able to develop a tone almost as good as the choir tone.

The kernel of the counter-tenor plan is that because of the type of training he has received as a soprano, the adolescent boy is able to keep his unchanged voice in use in the alto range during the period that the changed voice is emerging. The training takes care of the emerging changed voice, and the boy learns how to sing over the break, if there is one. The changed voice is not used in choir work while the boy is a counter-tenor; however, if he wants to sing tenor or bass, and can, he is transferred to the men's section. One thing the counter-tenor plan has demonstrated is that the boy can keep his unchanged voice in use for alto work much longer than has generally been thought possible.

In the grade schools, boys are trained to use their voices as Mr. Dorr trains his sopranos, but the training is not so intensive. The policy in the alto-tenor plan, on the other hand, is to encourage the voice to lower once adolescence starts. Because of this, the range at every stage of the adolescent period is a short one. In the counter-tenor plan, the method of training enables the boy to have a much wider alto range than in the alto-tenor plan; hence it is very practical for choir purposes, but not so practical for school conditions because of the time the more intensive training requires.

· 14 ·

The Junior Choirmen's Class at St. Mark's, Philadelphia

At St. Mark's Church, Philadelphia, H. William Hawke, while he was organist and choirmaster there from 1929 to 1945, tackled the problem of dealing with boys' voices during the adolescent period by running a junior choirmen's class analogous to that of treble probationers. Known as the Minton Pyne Singers,[1] the class was started primarily as a church effort to retain the interest of the boys after they had to leave the choir. Their ages were from about sixteen to twenty-one. The class never numbered more than twenty-four, for as new boys were admitted each year, a few left because they went to college or their work prevented them from keeping up their membership, and others got positions in other choirs.

In organizing the class, Mr. Hawke said he had no thought of its being of any value to the choir of St. Mark's Church, for the seating accommodation in the chancel for the men's sections was limited; consequently, there was no room for young men with immature voices. The eight men who could be accommodated had to be experienced singers with mature voices, able to prepare in one rehearsal a week the type of music used.

As Mr. Hawke explained, although the boys could no longer be used as altos in the choir, they "had a good deal of musical ability, and they had developed habits of church attendance. It seemed a pity to let these two factors go to waste. As it turned out, some boys developed so well that it was possible to take them into the regular choir as tenors or basses. It all worked out to the advantage of the choir work, for these young men were familiar with a great deal of the repertoire and its interpretation through having sung it as boys."

St. Mark's Choir consisted of twenty-four boy sopranos, eight boy altos,

[1] The class was named after a former organist of St. Mark's Church who came from England to America in 1881. He was considered one of the foremost church musicians of his time in the United States. He was a brother of Dr. J. Kendrick Pyne (at one time organist of Manchester Cathedral), who was a pupil of S. S. Wesley.

four tenors, and four basses. To keep the soprano section up to quota, a group of five to six probationers was selected at the beginning of each new season. Because of the difficulty he had in finding male altos and because he considered that the male alto tone did not blend with that of boy sopranos, Mr. Hawke started to use boy altos soon after he came to St. Mark's. He did not agree with the idea that the boy's voice should be rested during adolescence. "A boy in his teens uses his voice much more violently in his games than in any singing he could ever possibly do, and, as a rule, his voice is not harmed if it is not used too frequently in this unnatural manner. Hence in my own mind I have had to disregard all theory about absolute rest. But I do think rest is necessary in some cases, for example, if a boy has not the mentality to control his voice or adapt himself to the changing conditions. The problem in school is entirely different; results are not expected in such a short time as between one Sunday and the next, all the year round. The choirmaster has a certain number of hours in which to prepare the music for Sunday services; everything has to be planned out beforehand to the last minute, even to the number of minutes that can be spent on certain details in the compositions. Consequently, the work of the rehearsal must be done on schedule. In school, there can be interruptions, but as a result, any music that is being rehearsed is not much nearer the finished state than it was at the beginning of the rehearsal. Then too, in school, rehearsal time can be spent on experimentation. I should imagine that the alto-tenor plan is better for schools, but in choir work there cannot be too frequent changing of the boy's classification. I have competent men for the tenor and bass parts. I also have a smaller number of boys to work with and a larger repertoire to maintain, so that from necessity I have to keep the adolescent boy's voice at a static level for a longer period. Vocal training has to be done before and after rehearsal if any individual work has to be given a boy. That is why I have boys in small groups frequently; but I also work with them individually. I aim to take as many as possible each week before a rehearsal. I am at the piano an hour before a rehearsal and take the boys as they arrive. However, I do not make a regular schedule of this."

The rehearsal schedule for the week was as follows:

Mondays—Sopranos for one hour; Tuesdays—Altos for one hour; Wednesdays—Sopranos for one hour, sometimes with Altos; Thursday—Altos for one hour; Fridays—Full Choir for one hour and forty minutes.

THE BOY ALTO SECTION

A boy was considered ready to be transferred to the alto section if he found the highest notes of the soprano part difficult to sing. Also taken into account were his age and physique. Boys of thirteen to fifteen years of above average physique were transferred. One thing Mr. Hawke insisted on was that to get a place as an alto, a boy must have musical intelligence, and he must be able to read the average alto part with ease. Mr. Hawke attributed the success he had with his altos to the fact that he was able to attract to the choir a goodly number of musical boys; and because he was able to keep the section up to the quota of eight, there was never any necessity for an alto to force. If a boy was a good reader and had been assigned to second soprano parts, Mr. Hawke was inclined to put him in the alto section sooner than he normally would have, provided there was new material ready for the soprano section. One year, for example, the following three older boys were transferred from soprano to alto:

Case A was a fat overgrown boy of sixteen, with no signs of adolescence in his appearance. He could still have been used as a soprano. It was expected that he would have been able to sing alto for a year and a half at least; he was of the type physically that might become tenor. The boy did not remain in the choir, but he became a tenor as an adult.

Case B was tall and thin, thirteen years of age, and he was growing normally. He had been in the soprano section three years and had done solo work. He had always had rich lower notes and could have been called a mezzo soprano from the time he joined the choir. His speaking voice, too, had always had a rich quality. He could sing high A flat in chorus, and even in a solo, though not so satisfactorily just before he was transferred to alto. His voice developed into a fine bass.

Case C, an Italian boy and an excellent musician, was advanced for his age in every respect. It was not expected that he would be in the alto section for a complete season as it was evident that his voice was changing quickly. He got a position as tenor in the Roman Catholic Cathedral in Philadelphia while attending college, but it was thought that his voice would become baritone when it settled.

A boy was not kept singing alto once he developed a certain coarseness of tone in the lower notes and had difficulty singing the scale of B flat (soprano clef) descending. Mr. Hawke defined the coarseness thus: "A boy, as a soprano, has been trained to bring his head voice down. Singing alto he finds it impossible to retain the same production as he grows older, so he slips into chest production, thus causing a coarseness in the tone. But some boys do not have this difficulty."

A "mixed" tone was the aim in the alto section. Said Mr. Hawke, "The sopranos are trained to develop a light, graceful tone, working from 'uh' (as in *the*). When I consider a boy ready for the alto section, I begin to round out his tone by using 'oh' as a basis for all vowels; that is to say, the thinner vowels EE, EH, and AI, are covered by the 'oh' tone. This is also the training I use with the Minton Pyne Singers. It results in getting a rounder and more mature tone than the flute-like quality of the sopranos. I call it a 'mixed' tone because it is obtained by the same production that is used by the sopranos, but it has the addition of the training which is the start of adult voice training. I have boys as old as seventeen singing alto in this way, and yet they are able to sing quite a good light bass without any loss of quality. The voices have to be nursed at times, and sometimes a boy has to be cautioned about the way he is using his voice in the matter of production." At rehearsals altos who were able to sing in their changed voices sang the tenor or bass leads before their part entered, changing to alto without any difficulty. Mr. Hawke did not object to this, for he found that those who could do it enjoyed the experience of using their changed voices.

Because the extreme range of the alto part in church music is $G_{,}$ to E', Mr. Hawke advises against vocalizing outside of this range, and he recommends that a sharp lookout be kept for any difficulty between E and F (treble clef). If any occurs, it should be considered a warning that a boy's alto days are over.

Commenting on the fuller tone of his altos compared with a group of boy altos in school, Mr. Hawke said: "It must be remembered that my boys sing much more often and with greater concentration. With a school group it is a case of boys having to sing as a matter of routine rather than pleasure. My boys come to the choir because they want to sing; at rehearsals they have a job to do, and they apply themselves assiduously."

Nothing specific was done in St. Mark's Choir towards applying any kind of definite technique to enable the boy to pass from the boy alto voice to the changed voice, as is done in the alto-tenor plan or in the counter-tenor plan, the reason being, Mr. Hawke explained, that he had no room for adolescent tenors and basses in the choir. "I do not try to join up the boy voice to the changed, because I do not need to; and circumstances make it better for me to give the boy a rest before using him in the Minton Pyne Singers, unless in exceptional cases. The rest, however, is not a necessity, but a help to me in my plan. Rehearsals for the season do not begin until November. Thus a boy, who is no longer useful as an alto at the end of a season, rests his voice from June to November—longer, if he has had to stop singing alto during a season. I prefer not to admit boys to the Minton Pyne Singers during the season. I am not prepared to say, therefore, whether it would be better for the boy to sing through the changing period or not, for I have never tested this; and it would have been of no purpose to me to seek the opportunity to test this as far as my work was concerned."

It might be pointed out, as it has been elsewhere in this study, that those altos who sing the tenor and bass leads in rehearsals are helping themselves in the matter of joining up the unchanged to the changed voice, and in a natural way; and they are probably doing more for themselves than could be done under the discipline of a definite special procedure.

THE MINTON PYNE SINGERS

The test for membership in the Minton Pyne Singers was ability to sing C (octave below middle C) with a light, manly tone. New members were at first classified as Bass I because in the male voice music used, the range of this part is a medium one, putting no strain on the voice. No attempt was made to predict what a voice was going to be until after a boy had been in the Singers for at least two months. "I find that after a boy has been singing alto he is able to sing lower in his changed voice than he will after vocalizing is done regularly and frequently," Mr. Hawke said. Once it was fairly certain what a voice was going to be, it was classified as Bass I or II, or Tenor II, but a boy was never classified as Tenor I until it was quite certain that the range and timbre of his voice were Tenor I.

Rehearsals were conducted as class singing lessons, the boys being seated around the piano, so that it was possible to hear the tone of the individual voices. Development of nasal resonance was the first thing worked for. Boys hummed the descending scale of B flat to "N" and "M" merged to "uh." The relative thinness of the vowels "ee," "eh," and "ai" was then explained, and these vowels were rounded out by using "ah," "oh," and "oo." Often rehearsals were begun by using vowels only, thus: Tenor I on "oo" for the higher notes and "oh" for the lower; Tenor II on "oh" and "ah"; Bass I on "ah" and "ai"; and Bass II on "ai" and "ee." Mr. Hawke claimed that this plan made the group a fine sounding chorus.

Because the Minton Pyne Singers had only a few opportunities to sing church services, secular four-part music was used almost exclusively. A good deal of unison material was also used for voice training purposes—music of the type of Vaughan Williams' "Let Us Now Praise Famous Men"; and rounds were found useful because of their range.

· 15 ·

The Choral Music Program at Oundle School, England

Oundle School, in the town of Oundle, Northamptonshire, England, is known to musicians as the school which performs the *B Minor Mass*. The school is one of the oldest of the English public schools, having been founded in the early part of the sixteenth century. The outstanding feature of its music program is that every aspect of it leads up to an annual performance by the whole school of one of the great oratorios. That the whole school takes part means a plan was evolved to take care of the adolescent boys' voices.

Two men—a great headmaster known as "Sanderson of Oundle" and the late Clement M. Spurling, the Director of Music—were responsible for making Oundle School internationally famous. Both started their work in the school at about the same time. Sanderson was headmaster from 1892 to 1922; Spurling was appointed Director of Music in 1891 on the recommendation of Sir George Grove (of dictionary fame), who was at the time Director of the Royal Academy of Music, London, where Spurling had been a student from 1886 to 1890. The music program that was developed in Oundle would not have been possible had it not been for the educational policy of its headmaster and the music director's vision of the vocal possibilities of boys during the adolescent period.

An enunciation of Sanderson's educational policy is to be found in the book *Sanderson of Oundle* (London, Macmillan, 1923).[1] This policy was, "in all subjects, and by every available means, to extend to all boys under his care the opportunity of mental and spiritual enlightenment which has been too often reserved for a select few." He wished the school to provide everything that could interest and inspire, so that "no germ of life, mental or spiritual, in any boy, should perish for lack of suitable soil."

[1] The book, written as a testimony to Sanderson, gives the story of his work at Oundle. Over fifty people who had been under him and who knew him well contributed to it.

This policy he also applied to music. Although he himself was far from being a musician, he saw great opportunities for music in the school chapel service. When he first became headmaster, he announced that he expected the whole school, and not the choir only, to sing the hymns at the services. This was an innovation, and the older boys at first resented it.

"It was out of this innovation that the idea of the non-choir grew." The non-choir was made up of those boys who could not be in the choral society because of their voice limitations during the changing period. "Even though a boy could not read music, it was insisted that he at least hold the music up with both hands during the singing, so that he would have the attitude of taking an intelligent part in it, and not be following the organ carelessly by ear . . . the boy would learn to read music to some extent by doing it. With the opportunity would come the knowledge, then some interest, and later real appreciation and enjoyment."

In 1932, Oundle had its own chapel for the first time. This was one of Sanderson's visions, dating back to 1917, "when at a representative meeting of friends of the school, it was decided to erect a school chapel as a memorial to those Old Boys who had fallen in the Great War." The choir, which formerly had been made up of a small group of selected voices, was enlarged to nearly half the school. Music was chosen so that it would suit not only the choir but also the non-choir, and the non-choir had its own definite portion of the service to sing. The part that it took in the services constitutes one of the landmarks in the history of the music program. Two other landmarks were the founding of the choral society and the first performance by the whole school of *The Messiah* in 1921. The "whole" school comprised the choral society, the non-choir, and the orchestra.

The music program, however, was not confined to singing. "Sanderson knew the fundamental truth that music as a collection of pleasant sounds is nothing. He wanted the inner meaning which must be there. . . . It was not his wish that every boy who learned an instrument should necessarily become a competent performer. He aimed rather at using the instrumental teaching to extend knowledge and appreciation. He was never content with a realized advance. It must always be the starting point for another step."

Up to the time of his death, Sanderson had been working at a plan to include music in his "library scheme," a project he had used successfully with other subjects. To him a library had two purposes, a less and a greater: "the less was to obtain facts or verify them; the greater to endeavor by its means to find the answer to some question, to answer some problem of importance, such as, the worthiness of some form of art; the influence of a great musician upon his generation; whether or not a composer truly reflected the spirit of his time." Hence, the school came to have a large and comprehensive library of phonograph records and books about music. "I am not afraid to place in the hands of a young boy a book (or a record) which is beyond his comprehension," Sanderson was in the habit of saying.

THE NON-CHOIR IN THE MUSIC PROGRAM

According to Mr. Spurling's description of the school and its music program [2] in the 1920's, the total enrollment was around 580 boys, and there were two choral organizations, a choral society of 250 and a chapel choir of 300. The chapel choir was composed of one hundred trebles, approximately eighty to one hundred altos and tenors, and one hundred basses. The members of the choral society were selected from the chapel choir. Of the other choral group, known as the "non-choir," Mr. Spurling says: "What about those boys who cannot sing treble, alto, or tenor, and who are not yet ready to sing bass because they cannot get above middle C? Some of them perhaps cannot even get as high as this note, and moreover they have very little tone downwards from middle C in the bass. Shall these voices have a rest? Must these boys sing not at all? They simply cannot be prevented from using their voices in all kinds of ways. Listen to them in their leisure, or when shouting in support of their school at football matches. If their voices are going to be hurt at all, they are being hurt in these ways. Compare the harm done, if any, with that done to their voices singing in an orderly manner a part suitable to the compass of the voice which is theirs. In the latter we hear no shouting, no forcing of notes outside of a boy's true compass, and hence there is no straining of the voice, whereas on the other hand it is no uncommon experience for a voice to be quite hoarse after a good shout. But if we use these voices, are they effective, is the result satisfying musically, or is it not a mere raucous shout? The smaller the numbers the less effective broken voices can be, but throw the weight of two hundred and fifty of them in a four- or a five-part chorus and the effect is intensely fine. There is no raucous tone and nothing in the least distressing to the most musical ear."

The part that the non-choir has had in the chapel service can be seen

[2] Most of the quotations which appear in the balance of this chapter are taken from two articles by Mr. Spurling: "The Boy's Voice," *Dominant* (London), December 1928; and "Music in the Public Schools of Today," a paper read before the Musical Association of England, November 8, 1927, published in the *Proceedings of the Musical Association of England,* No. LIV, 1927.

from the following quotation: "Every boy in the school has a copy of whatever music is sung in the chapel service—chants, hymns, settings of the canticles, and anthems. Every boy sings in every part of the service—and this is one of the ways he learns to read music. At the weekly full practice (for the whole school) for the services, the non-choir is often rehearsed alone in its part, which may be a tune—sung an octave lower of course—or a special part. At times the trebles will sing a descant against the rest of the school singing the tune in unison. Wholehearted singing is expected from every boy and, if necessary, insisted on. Probably a small percentage of boys can never hope to get near a tune, but inability to sing is not admitted for one moment. The wrong notes of the few do not matter in the least among the right ones of so large a number of voices."

In the preparation of the large choral works for the Christmas concert the schedule of rehearsals, over a twelve-week period, was as follows:

Chorus and Non-Choir	10 minutes (after short prayers) three mornings a week
Trebles alone	One hour weekly
Altos alone	One hour weekly
Tenors and Basses together	One hour weekly
Chorus	One hour weekly
Orchestra	One hour weekly
Entire school with orchestra	Six hour-rehearsals

"It is at these practices that consciously and subsconsciously the boys lay a sure foundation in reading music. It is here that many boys who do not know whether they care about music or not—because they have never been given the chance or opportunity of taking part in it—learn to love enthusiastically and intelligently the greatest treasures of art; it is here that there are practically no boys who are not eager to take hold of the good things when these are offered to them attractively; it is here that they learn to sing with strenuous endeavor and to work with enthusiasm and vitality. They learn too, what it means to attempt a big difficult thing for the sheer love of doing it."

In the programs of the oratorio performances, there was always a footnote stating that the whole school (except the boys in the orchestra) was expected to sing certain excerpts; that is, the non-choir was to join with the chorus in these excerpts. Mr. Spurling supplied some typical examples (given below). It will be noted that they are usually the important themes which lie within a short compass rarely exceeding D to D'. Of these passages, he says: "When the non-choir sings with the trebles, it sings an octave lower of course, sometimes two. I give it a very large and important part in order that it may be constantly on the alert and ready to join the moving train." [3]

Excerpts from *The Messiah* (Novello Edition)
in Which the Non-Choir Joins

"And the Glory of the Lord"
  p. 10—Bass
  p. 12—Bass, bottom score, measure 3 to p. 14
  p. 17—Soprano, final last four measures
"Hallelujah Chorus"
  p. 150—Bass, measures 1 to 3 "for the Lord God Omnipotent reigneth"; also when the basses sing these words again on pp. 150 and 151
  p. 155—Tenor, bottom score, last two measures "King of Kings" to "Lord of Lords" at measure 2, p. 156; then join in the bass "and He shall reign" to "ever" on p. 157, middle score, measure 1; then to soprano part to the finish

Excerpts from the *Mass in B Minor* (Schirmer Edition)
in Which the Non-Choir Joins

"Kyrie Eleison" Chorus I
  p. 5—First entry of the fugue subject in the bass "Kyrie" to "eleison" (second score), measures 1 to 3 (first score), "Kyrie eleison" being sung an octave higher
  p. 8—Bass, measure 3, "Kyrie" to p. 9 bottom
"Sanctus" Chorus No. 20
  p. 163—Bass, measures 1 to 3
  p. 172—Bass, measure 4 to "terra" on p. 173, measure 5

In the *Mass,* Mr. Spurling reported there was never sufficient time to prepare the "Confiteor unum Baptisma" and the "Osanna," but at the performance all the other numbers were sung. In the *Christmas Oratorio* the non-choir sang with all the basses and tenors in the *da capo* of the bass solo, "Mighty Lord" (there are not many solos, he said, that make a greater appeal when sung by a unison chorus).

THE OUNDLE PLAN OF DEALING WITH THE CHANGING VOICE

Summing up the Oundle plan of dealing with boys' voices, Mr. Spurling says: "The altos are recruited from the trebles, and the tenors from the

[3] *The Oundle School Commemoration Booklet, 1933* gives the following information: "At the *Elijah* performance, December 18, 1933, the chorus numbered 191 trebles, 35 altos, 23 tenors, and 96 basses. The non-choir numbered 330. The soloists were . . . all well-known artists. Nine well-known orchestral players from London assisted the orchestra; a few visitors helped as singers or players. In all other respects the performance was the work of the whole school."

altos before their voices break. Sometimes an alto goes straight to bass although his voice has not yet cracked, but merely gone low. When the voices break, however, they join the boys in the non-choir, and the basses are recruited from the non-choir." In saying he recruited "the tenors from the altos before their voices break," he explained that when he used altos as tenors, this should be done at the right time, neither too soon nor too late. "This is before they have changed to bass and not before they have ceased to be able to sing alto; and before they have got a tenor compass." In other words, the Oundle plan is akin to our alto-tenor plan.

That there is a necessity for a classification, such as our alto-tenor, is evident from the following: "After the age of fourteen our trebles are tested again. We discover that some of them sing comfortably from middle C to its octave above, but that above this, there is a pronounced weakening of tone and a dislike to sing higher. On the other hand, they carry their thin register notes down to G below middle C, producing good round tone. These trebles are now ready to sing alto, but they must be watched for forcing the tone on the lowest notes as they gradually come to use their thick register. In a year's time or perhaps less, they are tested again. We make the discovery that A (soprano clef) is there, but that the notes above this have all but passed out of their compass, whilst the compass now extends downward to D (bass clef); that is, the range is d to A. There is no sign of a crack on middle C or any other note near C, but the thin register notes have now gone altogether; the boys can sing an octave and a half in their thick register with good strong tone. Useful as tenors? Very; they sing the high tenor notes with ease and brilliance, and these notes are most effective."

Mr. Spurling made it a policy to retest those voices which he had been using as tenors every three or four months, for "those whose voices break are of course no longer tenor. With a small percentage the voice does not break; it merely goes down and passes into the bass compass with ordinary tone."

Speaking of the effects of vacations on the boy's changing voice, Mr. Spurling says: "I think if our boys had no vacations and were to sing continuously, their voices would behave differently; but during two vacations of four weeks each and one of seven weeks, certain voices do not descend from treble to the man's bass without a break because they are not continually singing. This is especially so after the long vacation. A boy's voice has sometimes not just passed down, but it has a very definite break. The boy cannot be sure of even speaking normally; his voice is out of control." Further in connection with the break, Mr. Spurling draws attention to the fact that "some boys after the age of fourteen and a half develop a distinct crack in their voices which can only be detected with some care. They apparently sing with their thin register treble voice, but in reality, it is the falsetto voice. The crack will be noticed only by making them force the tone when singing middle C and below. If a crack has developed, middle C will show it."

The attitude in Oundle towards the traditional theory about the boy's voice is stated thus: "There is a great deal of scepticism with regard to the usefulness of boys' voices after they have left the ranks of the trebles, or at all events after they have finished with the alto part, and still more with regard to the kind of tone one can get from boys' broken voices. That the boy's voice, when it has broken, must of necessity be useless, or if used, can only produce a raucous, distressing, unmusical tone, is a fallacy. The statement is born of ignorance; so is the talk of ruining the voice if the boy is allowed to use it after it is broken and before it has settled. Probably it will not be really settled until after twenty years of age. There is complete uncertainty, of course, at what age the voice will change, but experience gives us this fact—the break seems to be delayed longer in the case of boys who have sung treble regularly from ten to fourteen years of age than it is in the case of boys who have been only listeners or who have done but little singing."

By "broken" it is quite evident that "changing" is meant. At the time the article was written, the term "broken" (or "cracked") was in common use whether a boy's voice broke or not. Had the article been written some years later, no doubt Mr. Spurling would have used the term "changing," in view of the change of attitude towards the boy voice question in England, especially in educational circles.

In a discussion on the paper Mr. Spurling read before the Musical Association of England in 1927, it was asked how balance was obtained from the choral society in which the altos and tenors were so few. Mr. Spurling replied that he did not care about certain things so long as he could get every boy to take part in the singing. "If the parts do not balance, I do not mind. As a matter of fact they do balance in the most extraordinary way. I have a few masters who sing bass and three or four who join the tenors, but I am independent of them. . . . I will not cut down the basses because they are too strong. I try to make the performance as good as possible. I am not preparing a performance of the *Mass* which I want the whole world to hear; I am preparing it because I want every boy to learn the *Mass*."

Having heard the singing of the Oundle choral society only from recordings, I asked Dr. R. Vaughan Williams, the English composer, for his impressions. He has permitted me to quote him as follows: "I heard the Oundle boys sing the *B Minor Mass* some years ago. I was much impressed and moved by the performance, but of course it was the spirit that impressed me, not the actual tone, though this was probably as good as could be expected from boys of their age."

· 16 ·

Choral Singing in a New Zealand High School

In *An Experiment in School Music-Making* by Vernon Griffiths, issued in 1941 by the New Zealand Council of Educational Research, there is described a plan for dealing with adolescent boys' voices that is used in the King Edward Technical College, Dunedin, New Zealand. The book is a report on the music program Dr. Griffiths developed in this two-year high school. "When the organization of a school program was begun in 1933," writes Dr. Griffiths, "there was no music of any kind at the daily assembly. No hymns were sung, no songs, and there was of course no band or orchestra. One teacher on the girls' side gave her students short intervals of singing during the class lessons; otherwise there was no organized choral work, no voice production, and no concerted singing." By 1941 the school had an orchestra, a band, and choirs that together included every student in the school.

BUILDING A TRADITION

Dr. Griffiths started his task with the conviction that if "music is organized on the bedrock foundation of practical music-making in choirs, orchestras, and bands, music appreciation and theory are never considered as separate subjects. Upon that foundation is built the superstructure of ear, voice, eye, and hand training, and, as the need arises, music appreciation and theory are introduced." [1]

[1] The quotations in this chapter are reprinted by permission from Vernon Griffiths' *An Experiment in School Music-Making,* copyright 1941, and published by the Oxford University Press, London, for the New Zealand Council of Educational Research.

Before he went to New Zealand, Dr. Griffiths had been music master at Downside School, near Bath, England, and later at St. Edmund's School, Canterbury, Kent. In 1927, he was appointed Lecturer in Music at the Teachers' Training College, Christchurch, New Zealand. In 1933, he was asked to organize a music program at the King Edward Technical College, Dunedin, and in 1942, he returned to Christchurch as Professor of Music at Canterbury University College.

As the school was a two-year one, Dr. Griffiths realized that to carry out his program, namely, "to build the foundations of a choral-singing tradition upon which the school hopes to build in the future," traditional methods of procedure must be discarded if other ones could be found to produce results in a shorter time. Hence, in the development of the choral program the assembly singing was made the starting point. Unison songs (sea chanties, national songs, and folk songs) were used. At first the singing was "self-conscious, toneless, and dispirited, as was to be expected. Enthusiasm had to be created. A choir of forty girls was organized; they rehearsed after school, and their first duty was to learn the assembly music so that they could give a lead to the rest of the school. Good tone was considered as the first essential; so stress was laid on this. Though a great deal of the music was learned by rote, some definite work was done in learning to read from notation. With the boys a different starting procedure was followed. A group was selected from the first year classes to present an operetta. The aim was to capture the interest of the boys of the school. Tone quality was made the selling point of the project, and though no definite work was done in learning to read the music—for it was learned by rote—every boy taking part in the operetta had a copy of the music. Out of these beginnings the choral program developed. The main foundation, the creation of enthusiasm, had been laid; from the first, interest had been centered in the work of the group rather than in the individual; systematic voice production and sight-reading had been begun; the daily assembly had become enlivened by the introduction of vocal music in addition to instrumental."

SIGHT-READING METHODS

As to sight-reading, Dr. Griffiths said the situation in his school was this: "The average length of stay in the school is under two years. Very few of the new pupils arriving each year from the elementary schools have had any real training in sight-reading. In a period of perhaps eighteen months these pupils have to be interested in music, if possible to the point of enthusiasm, and as many as possible must be induced to join the various instrumental and vocal groups. Music for the assembly, for concerts, and for other occasions, must be prepared and must reach a satisfactory standard of performance. It is obvious, therefore, that the sight-reading methods employed cannot be of the leisurely and round-about type." He refers to Arthur Somervell's *The Compleat Teacher* (London and New York, Boosey and Hawkes, 1934) as presenting one of the most practical methods he knows. (The virtue of this book is that it stresses the "mental effect" aspect of reading music.) "The system adopted in Dunedin has two main features. First, it is based on the music being studied in the instrumental and vocal classes, and in the orchestra, band, and choir. Second, it deals only with staff notation. Solfa syllables are employed and some use is made of the French time-names, but from the first it is the staff notation that counts. The purpose of sight-reading is to read staff notation at sight, not to be able to give any special name to any given note. . . . The basic essentials are (*1*) that the notation should always be associated with the actual sounds, preferably the sounds of the instrumental or choral music under rehearsal, the sounds coming first and the notation afterwards, and (*2*) that the system of instruction should be intelligently graded, one step leading logically to another."

THE ADOLESCENT BOY IN THE MASSED CHORUS

The plan of dealing with the adolescent boys' voices is described in Dr. Griffiths' chapter on choral music. "The choral work is built round three choirs, the massed choir, the concert choir, and the girls' concert choir. The massed choir consists of six sections—four of trebles and two of adolescent male voices. The first three treble sections are recruited entirely from the girls; the fourth is a mixed group which includes not only the remainder of the girls but also all the boys with treble voices. In effect, practically the whole school is drafted into this choir, the only pupils omitted being a small group of boys with so defective a sense of pitch that little can be done for them in the time available." [2]

The adolescent male voices of the massed six-part choir were divided into two groups, first and second, each of which rehearsed once a week in school time. Particular attention was given to tone production and to an intelligent understanding of staff notation. The range of the male voices was a, to d', and for the four treble parts it lay between B, and A'. The higher male voice group would correspond in America to Alto-Tenor II in a mixed voice group, and Bass I in the junior high school boys' glee club. The term "alto-tenor" is not known in New Zealand, but, as is evident, the alto-tenor stage of the boy's voice is taken care of.

[2] Dr. Griffiths informed me in March 1954: "The massed six-part choir now numbers eight hundred; it sings daily at Assembly. The massed orchestra numbers approximately three hundred; it consists of the Senior and Junior Orchestras, and the Senior and Junior Military Bands. All choral work is now concentrated in the six-part choir. The present director, Mr. Frank Callaway (who visited schools in America in 1949 and attended one of the Music Educators National Conferences), started his musical education at the age of twelve in my classes for children. He did his teacher training at the Dunedin Teachers' Training College; played in the local broadcasting orchestra and the band of the Royal New Zealand Air Force; and took over my work at the Technical College when in his early twenties, founding the King Edward Technical College Symphony Orchestra (consisting of advanced students who had left shool and a few other orchestral players who enrolled at the college to become members of the orchestra)."

THE DOMINION SONG BOOKS

Because of the lack of material to suit his plan of voice classification, Dr. Griffiths had to make six-part arrangements or compose original material in six parts. "As a rule, the tenor parts of published music are too high, and the bass parts, too low, for adolescent voices," he said. "Besides, the third and fourth treble parts demand very careful consideration in the matter of downward range, and for the fourth treble group, the part should be the easiest of the six parts." The majority of the boys' voices in the fourth treble group will change during the two years in school.

Dr. Griffiths was asked by the educational authorities to prepare for the Dominion Song Book series material to suit his voice classification ideas. By 1946, the following books, intended for adolescent voices, were published (Christchurch, New Zealand, Whitcombe and Tombs):

The Dominion Song Book, No. 8. Five hymns and seven folk songs arranged with bass tunes and descants for massed singing by four-part choirs of women and/or girls (three parts), and men and/or boys with broken voices (one part).

The Dominion Song Book, No. 10. Six folk songs arranged with a descant and a bass tune—four-part arrangements with free treble parts above the original melody, the melody being a bass for men or boys with broken voices. The book is intended for "choirs in post-primary schools, training colleges, and the various armed forces."

The Dominion Song Book, No. 11. Eleven folk song arrangements for male voice choirs (three parts), with optional descants for treble voices.

In the first two collections, the bass part is the melody of a folk song or hymn. In the third, the three lower parts are intended to be used by men or by boys with changing voices, or by both men and boys. The parts lie between $a_{,}$ and g'. "Separate the men into three groups in accordance with the natural range of their voices—high, middle, low," recommends Dr. Griffiths in his foreword. "Secure the best balance possible. Probably the high group will be numerically the smallest; and for satisfactory balance it will be necessary to secure good volume and really confident singing in the middle and low groups, both of which should be larger than the high group." The range of the descant for treble voices is D flat to F'.

Since 1946, the following books for adolescent voices have been added to the Dominion Song Book series: *No. 12*—hymn tune arrangements with the tune in the bass, similar to *No. 10; No. 13*—six original compositions (three by Dr. Griffiths and three by a colleague) for Trebles I and II, and Men I and II, the men's parts being for changing voices and amateur adult capabilities; and *No. 14*—a collection of hymns arranged so that they

From *The Dominion Song Book, No. 10,* by Vernon Griffiths (Whitcombe and Tombs, Ltd., Christchurch, New Zealand, 1944).

f
This song shall pass A - long this jov - ial ring — Let
this the bur - den of his song For ev - er used to be — "I
song shall pass from me to thee, A - long this jov - ial ring — Let
heart and voice and all a - gree — "Long live the
Verse (1) only
care for no - bo - dy, no, not I, If no - bo - dy cares for me."
heart and voice and all a-gree To say "Long live the
Verse (1) only

Verse (3) only
Much slower
King! Long — live the King!
King! Long live the King!
Much slower
Verse (2)
Fa la-la-la la, fa 1. la.
TREBLES (1), (2)
Fa la, fa la-la-la la, fa la-la-la la.
TREBLES (3)
Fa la, fa la-la-la la, fa la-la-la la fa la.
MEN
When spring be-gins its gay ca-reer Oh! how his heart is gay! No
Sum-mer drought a-larms his fear, Nor Win-ter's sad de-

2.
la.
No cares mar his joy Who doth sing and
la. No cares mar his joy, Who thus doth sing and
la. No cares mar his joy Who thus doth
- cay. No cares mar the mil - ler's joy, Who thus doth sing and
say — Fa la I live from day to day.
say — Fa la Fa la, fa la - la I live from day to day.
say — Fa la, fa la, fa la - la-la la, I live from day to day.
say — Let oth - ers toil from year to year, I live from day to day.

can be sung (*a*) in unison, (*b*) in unison with descant, (*c*) two-part (S.A.), (*d*) three-part (S.A.B.), or four-part (S.A.T.B.). Also published by the Board of the King Edward Technical College, Dunedin, New Zealand, are the following arrangements from *The Messiah:* "Hallelujah Chorus" (six parts), "And the Glory of the Lord" (up to five parts), "Lift up your Heads" (up to five parts), and "Worthy is the Lamb" (six parts); and from Haydn's *Creation,* "The Heavens are telling" (six parts).

· 17 ·

Conclusions

It is evident in this survey of current procedures used in dealing with the boy's changing voice that all have proved to be practical as well as successful. Because of the prominence given to the alto-tenor plan, it might be asked: What are the special virtues of the alto-tenor plan as compared with other plans? Is it a better one than any of the others, and if so, why? In presenting the survey, the purpose has been to show that no one plan suits every boy's voice; that a knowledge and understanding of other plans may prove to be useful at times, especially in schoolwork.

In evaluating the plans, certain factors have to be taken into consideration, namely, the working conditions under which each plan is carried out, and the caliber of the boys being dealt with. Working conditions in the school are not comparable with those in the choir; in the school the training is not of the intensive kind that is necessary in the choir if boys are to continue singing during the period that their voices are changing; hence there is not the pressure in the school lesson that there is in the choir rehearsal to produce results from week to week. Preservation of the voice as it develops to the adult stage is the dominant aim of the school music teacher; and nature decides the rate of the process.

In the choir, the boys are a much more homogeneous group from the musical standpoint than they are in a junior high school class of any grade. In the latter, the group is as heterogeneous a one as it is possible to find; the boys exhibit a bewildering variety of abilities and backgrounds in music as well as attitudes towards it. In the choir, the boys are selected at an early age for their musical aptitude, and they have had three to four years of intensive training in choir work before their voices reach the changing stage. Hence they are better able to manage their voices and overcome the difficulties that are inherent in the mutation process than the boy in school who has not had the choir training. This is especially true in the counter-tenor plan, where the boy sings alto even though the changed voice has developed, often to a considerable extent.

Of all the plans the alto-tenor plan has been longest in operation, and it has been tested on a much wider scale than any of the others. Evolved to meet the voice conditions of boys in the seventh, eighth, and ninth grades in the general music lesson,[1] where only a limited amount of time can be devoted to singing, it has proved itself evidently in the standard of the choral work of the high schools of today in America,[2] and in the growth of the all-state choruses. Further, the experience provided young people in the junior high and senior high schools has made it possible for colleges to have choruses which are capable of performing the great choral masterpieces, as well as works by contemporary composers, with professional symphony orchestras.

In churches that have a multiple choir program, choirmasters who are familiar with what the junior high schools are doing seem to favor the alto-tenor plan over the others, for they follow the principles of the plan in dealing with the boys in their units for adolescents where only one rehearsal a week is feasible.

From the choral point of view, the junior high school class can be considered an adult mixed chorus in its kindergarten stage. The alto-tenor plan has made it possible to think of the class in this way, because four-part music of the S.A.T.B. type can be used from the seventh grade up. This would not be possible with the baritone plan, for the boy at the alto-tenor stage has to sing either alto or what he can of the bass part as "baritone"; nor would it be possible with the counter-tenor plan, for the boy sings alto, and he does not sing tenor until he is almost an adult. Obviously, the music that will be used at first with a seventh grade class will be simple chord progressions of the cadence type, later developed into short phrases.[3] Singing in four-part harmony is a new experience for the boy, and new experiences are of vital interest in the junior high school in any activity, for through them the student grows. This is a strong point in favor of the alto-tenor plan.

[1] "The General Music Class" is very adequately discussed in Chapter 3 of *Guiding Junior-High-School Pupils in Music Experiences,* by Frances M. Andrews and Joseph A. Leeder (New York, Prentice-Hall, 1953).

[2] In a recent pamphlet, "Know your Schools," giving information for parents and taxpayers of the Port Chester, New York, school district (published by the Port Chester Board of Education and the Parent-Teachers Council and Teachers' Association) it is stated that the junior high school has the following choral organizations: Glee Club, Boys' Glee Club, and Mixed Chorus; and in the high school, the following: *A Cappella* Choir, Freshman Mixed Chorus, Sophomore Mixed Chorus, Junior Girls' Glee Club, and Advanced Boys' Glee Club. Clement A. Barton, Director of Music, attributes the success of the choral program in the junior high school to the all-around program of the elementary schools, and similarly the junior high school program has made the high school choral program possible and popular with the students.

[3] Genevieve A. Rorke, *Choral Teaching at the Junior High School Level* (Chicago, Hall and McCreary, 1947), gives several examples of this type. The book is one that can be highly recommended for the way it deals with teaching procedure in the initial stages of choral work.

It should be pointed out that the best results in singing in the junior high school are heard in school systems where the pupils have been taught systematically throughout the grades to read music and sing artistically with good tone. However, that the standard of singing in many schools is not what it could be must be attributed to the poor quality of the teaching and the lack of understanding of the boy's changing voice rather than to the pupils' previous training in the grade school, especially in reading from notation.[4]

For the purpose of identification, the plans described in this book have been named according to the classifications that are given the voice for the period that it goes through the mutation process. All have one thing in common, namely, each follows the comfortable range policy; any plan that follows this policy is a safe one to use. Some are more suitable for quickly changing voices, for example the alto-tenor and the baritone plans; while others are more suitable for slowly changing voices, for example the cambiata plan. As quickly changing voices are always more numerous, it would seem that the alto-tenor and baritone plans should be the more widely used plans. Since the baritone plan does not make provision for the third part of four-part music for mixed voices, the alto-tenor plan is to be preferred if it is desirable to use four-part music rather than three-part of the S.A.B. type. The junior high school general music class being the heart of the music program, the alto-tenor plan is the most suitable one if the class is thought of as the kindergarten stage of the adult mixed chorus.

All the plans, except the counter-tenor, follow the policy of allowing the changing voice to lower gradually to the changed status. This accords with the boy's natural growth through adolescence to manhood. Therefore, the counter-tenor plan is not so suitable in school, for the boy of junior high school age wants to grow to manhood as quickly as possible, and the emerging of the man's voice is one of the indications of his growth. The counter-tenor plan, however, is very suitable for the all-male church choir, since it solves the problem of the alto section by ensuring a continual supply of voices for the alto part—adult male altos being so rare and as a rule unacceptable to most American choirmasters.

The non-choir and the six-part voice classification plans seem to bear little resemblance to any of the other plans. A knowledge of their *raison d'être,* nevertheless, may suggest ideas that might be tried when the plan

[4] The music reading problem in the junior high school is not an easy one to solve. Andrews and Leeder, in *Guiding Junior-High-School Pupils in Music Experiences,* devote considerable attention to the matter, and they give several specific ways of making use of whatever instruction the pupils have had before entering the junior high school (p. 157).

being used does not work with an individual voice. This sometimes happens in school. The non-choir plan was evolved to fit the philosophy of the music program in a boys' school where the whole school takes part in the annual performance of one of the great choral works. Its originator seems to have had in mind (subconsciously) something akin to a combination of the alto-tenor and baritone plans, for the non-choir is made up of boys who are no longer able to sing the alto part in the music used in the school program, and they are not yet ready for the tenor or bass parts. The function of the non-choir is to serve as a unison chorus to join with the main chorus in reinforcing a part that, for example, announces a theme in a fugal passage, provided the music lies in a limited range between D and its octave above. The non-choir sings at the same pitch, or an octave lower or higher, depending on what the part is. The range for the non-choir is the combined Alto-Tenor II and Bass I ranges of the junior high school mixed chorus, or the combined Tenor II and Bass I ranges of the boys' glee club. It might be noted here that in several recently published song books for junior high schools, the trend in the arrangements is to use a great deal more unison than hitherto.

In the six-part voice classification plan, the problem is that there is very little published material for it. The originator of the plan and his colleagues have been tackling the problem by arranging national and folk songs or by composing original numbers for the plan. Because of the lack of material, the plan is out of the question for American schools, but there is no reason why it would not work if there were available the amount of music that has been published for the alto-tenor plan. The classification of the boys' voices into fourth trebles, upper and lower changed voices, indicates the possibility of the development of the type of boys' glee club that has become so popular in our junior high schools.

In sum, it would seem that the alto-tenor plan is the best one for school purposes; that an understanding of the baritone and cambiata plans can be very useful in dealing with voices that do not conform to the general pattern during the change; that the counter-tenor plan is more suitable for choirs than for schools; and that a knowledge of the non-choir and the six-part voice classification plans might prove to be of value on occasion.

Permissions

The author acknowledges the following permissions to use quoted material:

American Book Company, New York, for quotations from *Conductor's Book,* Hollis Dann Song Series, by Hollis Dann, 1936; *Junior Songs,* by Hollis Dann, 1918.

C. C. Birchard and Co., Boston, for quotations from *Glee Music for Junior High School Boys,* by Robert W. Gibbs and Haydn Morgan, 1937; *Twice 55 Part Songs for Boys: The Orange Book,* 1927.

J. Curwen and Sons, Ltd., London, for quotations from *A Heritage of Song: A Song Book for Adolescent Boys,* by Robert McLeod, 1932.

The Diapason (Chicago), for quotations from "Handling Problems, Administrative and Choral, in Choir Work," by Donald C. Gilley (September 1941).

Expression Company, Publishers, for quotations from *Speech Training in the Schools,* by Marjorie Gullan, 1929, published by Evans Bros., London; E. P. Dutton, New York (distributed by Expression Company Publishers, Magnolia, Massachusetts).

Carl Fischer, Inc., New York, for quotations from *Troubadors: A Collection of Four-Part Choruses,* by Mae Nightingale, 1939; *Tunetime for Teentime,* by Irvin Cooper, 1952.

Ginn and Co., Boston, for quotations from *The New Fourth Reader* of the National Music Course, by Luther Whiting Mason and George Veazie, 1891.

The Macmillan Co., London, for quotations from *Sanderson of Oundle,* 1923.

Music Educators Journal (Chicago), for quotations from "The Junior High School Choral Problem," by Irvin Cooper (November-December, 1950).

Music Teachers Review (New York), for quotations from "The Young People's Choir," by Federal Whittlesey (Spring 1942).

Musical Association of England, for quotations from "Music in Public Schools of Today," by Clement M. Spurling, in *Proceedings,* No. LIV, 1927.

Musical Times (London, Novello; New York, H. W. Gray), for quotations from an editorial by Harvey Grace (July 1932).

New Music Review (London, Novello; New York, H. W. Gray), for quotations from the issue of July 1930.

Oxford University Press, London, for quotations from *Clarendon Song Book for Boys with Changing Voices,* by W. Gillies Whittaker, Herbert Wiseman, John Wishart, and W. Norman Mellalieu, 1935; *Singing: The Art and Craft,* by W. S. Drew, 1937; *An Experiment in School Music-Making,* by Vernon Griffiths, 1941; and "The Boy's Voice," by Clement M. Spurling, *Dominant* (December 1928).

Paterson's Publications, Ltd., London, for quotations from *Mixed Voice Choirs: Female Voice Choirs; Male Voice Choirs,* by Hugh Robertson, 1923.

Theodore Presser Co., Bryn Mawr, Pennsylvania, for quotations from *The Glenn Glee Club Book for Boys,* by Mabelle Glenn and Virginia French, published by Oliver Ditson, 1927; *When Voices Are Changing,* by William Breach, published by Theodore Presser Co., 1936; and *History of Public School Music in the United States,* by Edward Birge, published by Oliver Ditson, 1928 (rev. ed., 1937).

G. Schirmer, Inc., New York, for quotations from *The Chorus Book for Boys,* by Ella M. Probst and J. Victor Berquist, 1922, 1925.

Silver Burdett Co., New York, for permission to reprint "Great and Marvellous Are Thy Works," arr. by Leo R. Lewis, from the Beacon Series No. 161, 1901.

Whitcombe and Tombs, Ltd., Christchurch, New Zealand, for permission to reprint "The Miller of the Dee," from *The Dominion Song Book, No. 10,* by Vernon Griffiths, 1944.

Index

Date Due

1-27-58
JUL 14 '58
JUL 29 '58
DEC 4 '58
SEP 18 1970
APR 12 1971
JUN 14 1971
9-28-72
NOV 16 1973
SEP 28 1976
FEB 25 1981
MAR 13 1981
APR 14 1981
JAN 5 1983
APR 01 1990
OCT 13 1993

PRINTED IN U. S. A.

MT915 .M2 c.1
McKenzie, Duncan, 18 100106 000
Training the boy's changing vo
3 9310 00064105 8
GOSHEN COLLEGE-GOOD LIBRARY